RUSH TO WIN

An inside story of a young candidate's long-shot campaign for City Hall

Jim Richards

ACKNOWLEDGEMENTS

Many thanks to my wife Sherry Carter, who supported my many hours of writing, and tirelessly helped me with ideas and editing.

Also thanks to Kay Honeyman, one of my favorite instructors in the creative program at SMU who also served as story editor for this book.

Dedicated to my friend and political advisor, the late Enid Gray.

INTRODUCTION

This book is about a nine-month period thirty five years ago when I was one of the young political activist candidates for office who were able to run because of a successful voting rights lawsuit asking for single-member districts.

While the methods of communication are different today, the issues are the same and the messages are the same, but social media has changed the method of delivery. The issues of who is qualified, both through relevant experience and temperament, are still important. Budgets and related tax rates are still important. Land use regulation through zoning is still important. Mobility is still important. The amount of community input and oversight into the activity of police is still important.

In today's times, political polarization seems to have evolved into tribal mentality. A reminder of how better outcomes can be achieved when folks work together to achieve a consensus result rather than engaging in a knock-down, drag out fight with a perceived enemy can be instructive.

The more citizens involved in local and state politics and government, the better the outcome. Lacking citizen involvement, a vacuum results that is usually filled by the few with something to gain at the expense of many. Hopefully, this book encourages folks, especially the young who might otherwise not be involved, to get involved.

The facts as stated in this book are basically true. It is based on my recollections and interpretations of events during an on again, off again and finally back on-again campaign for local office in a major city. Some of the conversations are verbatim; all are correct in substance but given the time since, some probably should be prefaced with "It went something like this".

PROLOGUE

Crockett, Texas, June 2, 1945. Rebecca Richards had spent ten hours in labor before finally giving birth in a tiny hospital in this small town. She was in a large room that was set up for five patients with canvas screen dividers between each bed. The sheets, walls, floor, ceiling and furniture were stark white, giving the room an aura of being sterile, whether it was or not. In circa 1945 the combination of drugs used to relieve the pain of childbirth brought on vivid hallucinations, to which I hope attributed to the next conversation and not anything about me personally.

Rebecca was quickly awakened. "Mrs. Richards, here is your son that I believe you have planned to named Jim," said a beaming nurse as she attempted to pass me to my mother for the first time.

An exhausted Rebecca rose up in the bed with a dazed look on her face and exclaimed. "My God, that's the ugliest baby I've ever seen in my life! It can't be mine!"

"It's yours, Mrs. Richards. It's the only baby in the hospital," said the chuckling nurse as she made another attempt to pass me to my mother.

I didn't think it was funny at all, being rejected by my own mother on my first day on Earth. Not having learned to talk yet, all I could do was scream and scream I did. At that moment a neuronal chaos seeded a sprout of self-doubt in the brain of a rejected, screaming newborn. As far back as I can remember, I have felt I have something to prove.

A nineteenth century quote, from the prominent French jurist and academic, Anselme Polycarpe Batbie, refers to classical liberals as Republicans.

"He who is not a républicain at twenty compels one to doubt the generosity of his heart; but he who, after thirty, persists, compels one to doubt the soundness of his mind."

The quote over the years has evolved into: *"If you're under thirty and not a liberal, you have no heart. If you're over thirty and not a conservative, you have no brain,"* but the meaning hasn't changed.

As most young men and women growing up in East Texas, I was a Democrat. I like to say I was born a Democrat because both of my parents were Democrats, genuine liberal Democrats. Mother was a high school English teacher, who was raised by her conservative aunt and uncle in Sherman, Texas. She went to graduate school at what she called "The University," UT in Austin. It must have been those years in Austin that converted her. My father was an East Texas Yellow Dog Democrat, who said Republicans were for big business and that the Democrats were for the little man and for small business, and that description wasn't too far off in the 1950's and 1960's.

Sometime in those successive years the viewpoints of some conservatives evolve to a more moderate position on issues, and that's what happened to me. While I may be skeptical of increasing the size of government in general, I know how hard it is to take something away from anybody. Anyone who says "it's as easy as taking candy away from a baby" has never tried to take candy away from a baby. While people may not remember who gave them a government program, they will surely remember who took it away from them.

Many folks interested in politics in general have been less interested in municipal politics or municipal government. In their minds what matters most happens in Washington D.C. Next comes state governments where governors and legislatures preside. Cities and school districts were even below state government. They just weren't that important, especially since most of those elections were non-partisan.

That approach ignores reality. Municipal governments have more direct effect on citizens' everyday life than any other level. They provide streets and enforce the rules of driving. They keep the peace and put out the fires. They provide water and sewer services. They educate our children. They regulate land use so that someone doesn't build a high rise commercial building in the middle of a single-family neighborhood. They provide physical and mental health care for the indigent. Some of the effect on citizens is set by school districts and the county, but it's still local government.

As the result of a reform movement in the 1930s, many Texas cities, including Dallas, adopted the council-manager form of municipal government, as opposed to the strong mayor form one finds in most large cities in the U.S. In the council-manager system, a professional city manager is selected by a majority vote of the city council and manages the city bureaucracy. The city manager reports to the mayor and city council much like a corporate CEO would report to a board of directors. The mayor is the presiding officer over council meetings, serving much like a non-officer chairman of a corporate board.

For small cities, this type of government enables the mayor and council members to serve on a "part time" basis, much like being on the board of a local charity or other civic organization, except more time is involved. If one is serving part time, then they don't need a salary. Supposedly, this means that someone would only run and serve as a "civic duty." In addition, most municipal elections are non-partisan, in an attempt to keep partisan political activists out of municipal politics.

As the city of Dallas' population and development increased, the complexity and time required for serving increased as well, resulting in a situation where to serve well and fairly represent your constituents, you must either be (1) wealthy and/or retired, (2) own a business you can manage on a part time basis, or (3) have an employer allow you to work part time and serve part time. Many law firms tolerated associates or junior partners who wanted to run, since the exposure could good for the firm.

For many years, the Dallas Citizens Council, an organization composed of CEOs of major corporations, banks and law firms controlled local government. The Citizens Council was the establishment. In addition to the mayor of Dallas, all City Council members were elected at-large, or city wide, requiring a candidate to either be a local celebrity or have the ability to raise enough funds to create name recognition.

Members of the Citizens Council and the Chamber of Commerce were prime providers of those funds, allowing them to pick and choose candidates who would be successful with their help. Their chosen candidates were usually older men and women with backgrounds deep in civic involvement. Those candidates were known as reasonable, upstanding folks who wouldn't rock the boat as visualized by Citizens Council members.

In 1971 a federal voting rights lawsuit asking for single-member districts was filed, where a candidate could either be known within that district or able to campaign enough to win, even against an establishment backed candidate. As a result of that lawsuit, a plan was implemented in 1975 for single-member districts. Thus, racial minorities who were activists and younger, more politically oriented candidates who cut their teeth on partisan political campaigns emerged and began to run and win elections. Those newcomers changed the political discourse as they sought to represent folks who they believed were under-represented in the at-large election system.

African-American council members, who were hand-picked for so long by the Dallas Citizens Council gave way to more independent minded activists who spoke loudly about any issue they perceived to be an example of racial injustice, especially when it came to conflicts between members of their community and the Dallas Police Department.

There was another fight in the making, a conflict over land use. Dallas is a city encircled by suburbs, so its growth is more or less limited to increasing density of real estate development in areas where there is market demand for development. Dallas regulates its land use by zoning and if the density of development increases, properties usually require up zoning or increasing the "floor area ratio" or the per square foot of building divided by the per square foot of land. Other restrictions include the type of development allowed, i.e., single-family residential, multi-family residential, retail, or a type of industrial classification.

During expansion phases, up zoning makes a property more valuable, since it can be developed with a higher floor area ratio and thus more square feet of building per square feet of land. In many cases, adjoining single-family homeowners' properties either lose value or are perceived to lose value, because of the intrusion, and with it increased traffic and noise. Especially when multi-story office buildings are constructed close to residential neighborhoods and tenants of those buildings have full view into the backyards of neighborhood residents.

When the "investment of one's life" as the realtors like to say is threatened, political tension is created. Rapid growth and development can also result in clogged streets, overcrowded freeways, and overall gridlock. The part of Dallas where I had lived the longest, since moving there in the late 1960's, endured the brunt of many of those problems. As a result, homeowners began to band together, form associations and get involved in politics. They were even able to get some of their advocates elected, especially in the new single-member districts.

The third fight brewing was about taxes and spending. Some state constitutions allow for initiative and referendum on the state level, whereby citizens can petition the state for a state-wide vote on just about any issue. Proposition 13 that limited tax rates in California had recently passed and like many issues, trends start in California and drift eastward. Dallas had an anti-tax group called the Tea Party who ran candidates in both the single-member districts as well as the at-large, city wide districts.

This was the climate in Dallas, and many other Texas central cities, circa 1983 that were rich with opportunities for a guy born in a small East Texas town with something to prove.

IN THE BEGINNING

My friend, Alan Steelman, former Republican congressman from Texas, once told me, "Many politicians and erstwhile politicians say they pray to God for guidance as to whether they should run for higher office or not. It seems that God always tells them to run and never tells them not to run." I was going to make a huge life changing decision and didn't want to pray about it, fearing that the outcome, good or bad, may be preordained.

The first sign of my coming decision emerged as I was at Steve Bartlett's Victory Party after his tough primary race for Congress. The victory party was held outside the campaign headquarters on a huge patio. It was a cool, clear spring evening, and there was plenty of spicy Tex-Mex food to eat and cold beer to drink. Consumption of the former led to an increase in consumption of the latter to cool the palate.

Celebration was in the air as people were in a festive mood, joking and laughing with each other. Hundreds of people were in attendance, not all of whom supported Steve. These new converts were welcomed, since every good winner needs to consolidate their position. I had enjoyed the Bartlett campaign and poured myself into it. One of my functions was to work with the finance committee, give them encouragement and otherwise help as needed. I also built a grass roots organization in my area of North Dallas and ran the phone center a couple of nights a week.

I was trying to explain the political landscape in Texas to two of my new friends, transplants from out of state. We were standing together near the bar where l was greeting friends and co-workers as they walked by. My explanation to the two started with one of my favorite sayings, first attributed to Texas State Sen. Carl Parker of the Beaumont/Port Arthur, Texas area and later modified by me to fit whatever circumstances I found myself in. "In Texas politics, we don't lie to each other unless it's absolutely necessary."

One of the two friends, Bill Booher, a new resident of Dallas who was the public affairs director for Lone Star Steel was an accomplished pol himself. "Gee, Jim, I'm glad you told me that about Texas because I would have never guessed it," he jested.

My other friend, Fred Stern, had recently moved to Texas from Delaware where early in his career, he was a senior aide to Governor Pete du Pont with ambitions to be president when President Reagan's two terms were up. He asked, "What's an example of when it's absolutely necessary?"

"Why it has to be something of monumental importance, something involving money, sex or football, not necessarily in that order." With that, we three had a good laugh, separated and began working the crowd at the party.

The energy in the area was palpable. Like a sponge I soaked it in as I was fueled by the excitement. I realized just how much I enjoyed this. It was not only the excitement of the campaign but being involved in something bigger than me. I may have finally found my calling, as the preachers in East Texas used to say, except they claimed to be called by a higher power for a much higher pursuit.

Up comes Fred Meyer, the Dallas County Republican Party chairman. Fred was a cheerleader for his candidates and was always voicing the merits of the party and its platform and positions, an unrelenting optimist. He was there with his usual recruiting pitch for activists, positive and loud of course, "Jim, when are you going to run for something?"

"Why thank you, Mr. Chairman, for the compliment," I always addressed Fred as "Mr. Chairman" to show his due respect. "Maybe someday," I replied, as he turned to greet the next guest.

For the first time in over twenty years since my high school days, I was beginning to feel that same adrenaline charge I used to get from my perilous hobby, drag racing, usually on two-lane country roads, thankfully which had little, if any traffic at night. Since I hadn't experienced that kind of charge in a long time, I walked away from the party for a few minutes to find a quiet spot to be alone with my thoughts and for a moment, indulge myself in the past and relive the thrill of the drag race and what it meant to me. I lit a cigarette, took a deep breath in and closed my eyes, letting my mind wander back to 1962.

I'm a 17-year-old kid, a shade tree mechanic. A name that aptly describes a guy, usually a farmer, who is not a real mechanic but one who works on his pickup or tractor under the shade of a tree. One of the few places to find refuge from the searing heat of a hot summer day in Texas. I had transformed a 1957 Chevy Coupe into an ugly but powerful drag racing machine. We raced at the Tyler/Whitehouse drag strip outside of Tyler, Texas, a quarter mile strip on private property about an hour's drive from my home. The place was full of older cars modified for drag racing, as well as real rail dragsters, built from the ground up with no purpose other than to race. There's a grandstand (well, bleachers at least) on one side of the strip with a box looking wooden enclosure at the top for the announcers. The pit area is on the other side of the strip and that's where my buddies and I stood to watch the other races.

Finally, my number was called to line up behind a few other cars. The noise was deafening as my opponent and I pulled our cars out of the pits and lined up close to the starting line to wait our turn in the B Modified Stock category. The air was thick with fumes from the last several races, run by rail dragsters burning nitro methane.

My car's exhaust dumps were off so the exhaust fumes and the noise, of course, came right out of the exhaust manifold. No mufflers to dampen the sound. Little did I know that the loud noise would harm my hearing but, in the end, attributed to my failing my army physical and missing out on a year in Vietnam. I knew I would go home with a headache from the fuel vapors and the noise but didn't care.

We pulled up to the starting line. I loved the adrenaline rush of a race. My senses are heightened, and I was totally focused and aware of immediate surroundings. My vision and hearing were sharp. Concentration was at its height. Clutch in, gear box in first, accelerator more than half way to the floor. The old car shook from the vibration of an engine at 5,000 rpm at the starting line. The excitement level is sky high. Even though I had no idea who I was running against or how fast their car was, I knew the only way I could lose this race was to spin down at the start or miss a gear in a power shift.

My opponent and I watched the start signal change colors, red, yellow, yellow, and red, in a completely random order and then finally green. Tires screamed for traction, engines wailed louder as the accelerator stays on the floor. We change gears, with one eye on the track ahead, the other on the tachometer so to power shift at 6,500. I know if I passed 7,000, I could kiss my engine goodbye. The quarter mile race lasted only a few seconds and then it's over.

The adrenaline slowly fades and my heightened senses faded with it. I go back to the pits, ice down the intake manifold to help the fuel flow and wait for the next race. A beer can in one hand and a cigarette in the other. One of my buddies walks by. "What happened to you out there? I thought you could win that one."

I shrug. "Oh hell, I spun down and missed second." It was the perennial excuse for losing a drag race. You never, ever blame your car because while your car's capabilities are to your credit, its deficiencies are your blame to bear.

Drag racing on a drag strip built for that purpose alone is exciting but it doesn't match drag racing late at night on a two-lane country road. There is the race itself, but someone has to be in the wrong lane and at risk of a head on collision.

But at 17 I believed I was invincible. Now that's excitement, blind to the danger ahead. And of course, it was highly illegal.

"What are you doing standing out here alone in a daze?" My wife Jetta had left the party and was looking for me. She was miffed. "I've been looking for you for quite a while."

"I just came out here for a cigarette and a few minutes to reflect on the past and the future," Thinking about Fred's question, I changed the subject. "You know, being a volunteer campaign worker is fun but I want more involvement, something else. I would like to be able to make more of a difference."

The look on Jetta's face changed. Her lips pursed, and her eyes narrowed as she stood there staring at me, arms crossed.

"While many people don't like campaigning, I do. I've campaigned for a lot of other candidates and would like to be a candidate myself someday."

"You're not thinking about running now, are you? We have a child and a mortgage. Who would help you anyway?"

That was meant as wise advice, and it was but it was discouraging.

"Good question and one that I don't have an answer to."

"Well, maybe you should think about that."

"When my opportunity comes, I have to be ready to take it. Am I ready now? Who knows, but probably not." There was the time, the money, the risk of losing. Plus, the thought of public speaking had been scary in the past. I had spent the last few years in Toastmasters and was getting better at it. Those were reasons that I might not be ready. But there was also this feeling of excitement that I hadn't had since drag racing. That excitement moved me past doubts about not being ready.

"I've been building a support base of folks that I've volunteered with in political campaigns, civic work and my church. I'm trying to keep in touch with each one."

"I was afraid you were serious about this."

"Jetta, you know I love cities, especially this city, Dallas, I always have. Being from a small town, I'd always had a yearning for the city, part fire in my belly to make good." Her expression didn't change at all.

I tried another tact. "Like Chicago, Houston has broad shoulders. It's a blue-collar town, with the ship channel, chemical plants, and refineries. Dallas is technology, banking, insurance and corporate headquarters. Dallas has a heartbeat, a town full of energy with lots of deal making."

I'll never forget my first visit to Dallas. After I recovered from polio, my mother took my sister and me to the Texas State Fair in Dallas. The fairgrounds seemed to stretch for miles. I'd never seen a crowd that size. The air was thick with smells, sounds and sights that were new to me. The motto on the colorful banner above the gate of the fairgrounds was *"There's More to See in '53"* and there was plenty of attractions for an eight-year-old to see and remember.

"Jetta, I want to do something important, outside of work. I want to do something good for Dallas. I want to make a difference. Politics can be addicting. The more I'm involved, the more I want to do and the more yen I have to do something bigger."

"Just make sure you're financially independent before setting off on something crazy like that."

I knew she was right, but I couldn't get it out of my mind. Since growing up with politically aware parents, I've always been interested in history, public affairs and politics. I remember my cousin, George Howe Richards, who was a Texas State Representative from Huntsville, and how excited Dad and his sisters were when George came to town. He was a small guy with a big personality. He would regale us with stories of goings on in Austin when the Legislature was in session.

My interest in cities in general and Dallas in particular brought me where? Why would I want to run for something like the Dallas City Council and be subjected to endless questioning of motive, competence, morality, experience, and dedication as well as criticism, debate, and complaining, all for a job that requires a 40 plus hour work week schedule and pays fifty dollars a meeting? I was starting to see Jetta's side and could understand why she wouldn't want to subject our family to that.

President Lyndon Johnson told the story about himself watching a bull rider at the rodeo where his father took him as a kid. The story goes something like this. "My father let me get to a place in the arena where I could see the bull and the rider up close. Bull riding is dangerous business. The rider could get stomped, crushed against the wall or gored by the bull. Why does he do it? Why does the rider do it? When the bull turns so that the rider and the bull are facing me, I can see the fury in the bull's face and the valor in the rider's face. That's why he does it. It's fun, dangerous, and exciting!"

So, why run? Because I thought it would be a challenge, a new adventure, a mountain to climb, a long journey to complete, a way to prove myself.

During circa 1972/1973 my mother requested that I bring her an autographed copy of *The Best and the Brightest*, David Halberstam's book on the Kennedy and Johnson administrations and the Vietnam War. I bought the paperback for myself and read it a year or so later while being sequestered to bed for a few days recovering from the flu. I read the book cover to cover and was hooked. That book, watching the Watergate hearings, and paying attention to both national and local news casts piqued my interest. I started reading biographies of political leaders and decided there was more to life than working. I wanted to make a difference outside of my current world as I knew it. I wanted to be involved in something far reaching, beyond my current experience; to step outside the box and challenge myself. I wanted to be somebody that was in the action, not just on the side lines.

Daydreams over, I snuffed my cigarette and escorted Jetta back to the party. A festive atmosphere was still in the air, but many people had left by then. Jetta was right to be practical. It was a dream for another time in my life when I'm financially independent and before growing too old to do something meaningful beyond day to day responsibilities of work and family.

A pessimistic cloud hung over me and the winds of change weren't there.

OPPORTUNITY CALLS

The phone rang at 6:00 a.m. I managed a groggy "Hello," wondering who would be calling this early.

I recognized the voice. My friend Bill Booher was on the line.

"Wake up, Jim. I have an opportunity for you."

"What time is it?" I grumbled.

"Sorry, I'm in D.C. and forgot about the time difference. But this is important."

Little did I know how important this news was and that it had the potential to change my life.

"Go outside and get your *Dallas Morning News*, open to the Metro Section and call me back now!"

I followed his instructions; orders seemed to better describe his tone of voice. It was early June and the temperature was heading for another 100 degree day in Dallas. I grabbed the paper and went inside where it was cooler, sat down in a chair at the dining room table, spread the paper out and thumbed through to the Metro section. Even though the story was buried in the Metro, to my eyes it was front page, above the fold, in three-inch headlines. Joe Haggar was not seeking re-election. My mood was suddenly stoked by one of those drag racing adrenaline rushes. I think my heart skipped a beat. I quickly called Bill back.

"Hey Jim. Don't you live in Joe Haggar's City Council District?"

"How'd you know it was me?"

"So, you read the article?"

"Yeah, I live in the district. Why do you ask?" *I knew what he was implying but did I dare embrace the idea of running. Maybe his call was validation enough.*

"This could be real opportunity for you. Run and win, serve the traditional two, two-year terms and then aim for something else. State Senate, for instance. Ike Harris isn't going to be there forever."

"I do like the idea of non-partisan politics, which I take as bi-partisan because it's fun to work with friends on both sides."

"This seems set up for someone like you to run," Bill continued. "A young candidate who would represent the single-family homeowners in the district rather than the local real estate developers, many of whom live in the Park Cities, anyway."

I thought it's a perfect opportunity but then quickly returned to reality; my reality of needing to work full time. I was no longer a single guy living in a small apartment, but married, with a two-year-old child and a home mortgage. My cautious reply sounded as much like a question as an answer.

"It's, ahh...tempting?"

"You better move quickly. I've already heard a woman named Betty Svoboda is running."

"I'll think about it." I thought of nothing else for the next several days.

Luckily, I knew a man who knew Betty Svoboda, Jack Worley. Jack and I worked for the same company, Gulf United Corporation, where he ran the real estate operations which invested in raw land. Gulf United was not a developer, just a long-term investor of life insurance profits. Jack's office was right next door to mine. The next morning I found Jack in his office, having his morning coffee and organizing his day. His office walls were decorated with giant aerial photographs of farmland north of Dallas. He used them to try to put together all the contiguous farms he could buy in order to create a track of land, primed for development. Jack was also a past president of the North Dallas Chamber of Commerce.

"Jack, what do you know about Betty Svoboda? I heard she's running for City Council."

Jack's brow furrowed above his frown. "Betty is running. She's an ambitious real estate agent who works for Ebby Halliday. She has recruited Ebby to be her campaign chair. Betty's smart and hard working. She's made her reputation by putting together a crime watch organization in Northwest Dallas and has done a good job with that project. During the last couple of days Betty and Ebby have put together an executive steering committee, including all but one of the living past presidents of the North Dallas Chamber. They have a huge head start because they knew Joe wasn't running weeks before the official announcement. She looks formidable, but she might have competition."

"Who's the one hold out?" I asked.

"It's me." Jack said with a sheepish grin.

"Why you?"

"Because I know her."

"What do you know about her?"

"Well Jim, it's like this. Betty knows a lot about the City and City issues from her position with the crime watch organization and from serving on the Dallas Park Board. She's smart but the problem is her wisdom and social agility lag behind her intelligence. She doesn't suffer fools lightly and has a tendency to tell people what to do. Most people resent that. I don't believe Betty has the kind of personality one needs to be a good council member. She's not a good listener and not very receptive to what other people think."

That piqued my interest even more. "Okay, tell me about the Chamber. You must know a lot about it."

"The North Dallas Chamber is the closest thing to the establishment for the business community of North Dallas. They have a lot of power when they agree, and they agree on Betty. But the support has been driven by Ebby Halliday, a revered leader in the real estate community. She has recruited the supporters and raised the war chest to discourage others from running."

"How successful are they in winning local elections?" I asked.

"When united, they are virtually undefeated with folks they backed in local elections."

"But they don't have you." I knew I most likely couldn't run but the fantasy was strong.

"They must have been planning this for months." Jack leans forward and folds his hands together. "Are you thinking about running?"

I paused and looked past Jack. "I don't know. Maybe."

"Well, pray about it before you decide. Then let me know what you're going to do."

I got up and shook his hand. "You'll be one of the first to hear."

Over the next week or so I discussed the race with several friends, not knowing who would tell whom about my consideration. I wanted to do this but was still holding back. I doubted my ability to win but the larger issue was keeping my job at Gulf United.

The day after I met with Jack the phone rings at my office with a warning.

"Hello, Jim Richards," I answered.

The woman on the line had a stern voice that was teeming with determination.

"Jim, we've never met but my name is Betty Svoboda."

I stood up, then sat back down. She had my attention. Does rumor travel fast in this town or what?

"I heard you're considering a race for Joe Haggar's seat on the Dallas City Council. Forget about it, buddy. I'm going to run and you won't stand a chance. I've been on the park board. My supporters include several good friends who are active in the many Republican women's clubs in Northwest Dallas and I run the crime watch program in that same area. Finally, my campaign chair is Ebby Halliday, and everybody knows about her history of civic and political engagement. I have an executive steering committee composed of most of the past presidents of the North Dallas Chamber of Commerce."

Her words hit hard. Thankful for the long cord on my office telephone, I got up from behind my desk, walked over and closed my door and began to pace back and forth to ease a sudden onset of nervous energy.

"Is that right? Sounds like you've got the race wrapped up and it's only June." I said, emphasizing my East Texas country accent, which not only doesn't need much playing up, it also tends to disarm angry folks.

"And Betty, I'm so glad to get to finally meet you, at least over the telephone. I've been hearing a lot about you the last few days. Maybe I'll get to meet you in person soon."

Stunned silence on the other end of the line. *Maybe she's not used to common courtesy.*

After 30 seconds or so she resumed. "Well, you've been talking about the race. Are you considering running?"

"Betty, some people have suggested that I consider the race. I live in the district, meet the age qualifications, and I'm thinking about it. But the reality is I'm just a simple guy from a small town behind 'The Pine Curtain' in East Texas." *Now that's my country bono fides. Should make her doubt I'm much of a threat.*

"Don't give me that BS. My campaign has researched you and you're more than just a country bumpkin."

"So you think I'm qualified, great!"

My baiting didn't seem to rattle her.

"I didn't say that. Just remember what I said. You don't stand a chance, so don't waste your time."

Click went the phone line.

That telephone conversation sort of "upped the ante." Little did she know her call made me even more interested in running. I felt that same old adrenaline rush I used to get when challenged to a drag race.

Jack Worley suggested I pray about it. What am I to do and do I dare pray about it?

DON'T TAKE THAT CALL

The mass of men live lives of quiet desperation.

Henry David Thoreau

Lasagna was in the oven and the aroma permeated throughout the house. A few friends were coming over for dinner about a week after we got word that Joe Hagger wasn't running for re-election to the Council and his seat would be open. The first couple to arrive were Skip and Paula Pedlar.

Our home was built in the late 1940's. It had a small entryway between the living and dining rooms that led to a staircase. I opened the front door for them and felt the rush of the hot summer air. It was June and we still had the July and August heat to look forward to. Skip was a likable guy, a CPA with a local firm in Dallas who had been politically active with the Bartlett campaign.

Jetta liked the Pedlars, especially Paula, who always had something funny, insightful or both to say about people. She came out of the kitchen to greet them.

"Paula, let's go back to the kitchen for a glass of wine. Jim, take Skip into the den, where you both can sit down and relax." We had to walk through the kitchen to get to the den but Jetta either didn't hear or simply ignored what Skip was saying as we walked through.

"Jim, there's an open seat on the Dallas City Council calling for you. Your city needs you."

I'm thinking maybe the seat is calling for you Skip since you live in the district as well!

"You're on the merry-go-round of life and the carousel is approaching the point where you can grab the brass ring. You may never get another chance, so what are you going to do?"

Before I could reply the doorbell rang. *Saved by the bell, at least temporarily.* Bill Booher and his wife Liz, the other couple we invited, arrived for dinner. Liz, like Bill, had an upbeat and likeable personality.

After everybody greeted everyone else Jetta returned with Paula to the kitchen to check on the meal. Bill, Liz and I joined Skip in the den. I poured beer and wine for our guests. The four of us sat around a coffee table and sipped our drinks.

Skip resumed. "So, are you going to seize the opportunity and grab that brass ring or go through life wishing you had?"

"Skip, it's not that easy of a choice. Betty Svoboda has announced that she's running and Ebby Halliday will be her finance chair, if not campaign chair. It doesn't matter what position Ebby holds. Her name as the holder of any chair position or treasurer is enough to get Betty an overwhelming amount of support."

I continued. "Sure, Betty turns some people off. But she's smart, informed and a hard worker and will be tough, if not impossible with Ebby's help, to beat. She even called me the other day to discourage me from running. The woman was confident but also pretty abrupt with me. It was like her call to me and our conversation were on a list of things she had to do so she could check it off her list. It wasn't personal at all. She must be used to telling other people what to do, even if she has no authority over them."

Skip shrugged, "Yes, she's a formidable candidate even without Ebby, but you're a young business guy who could represent the neighborhoods. People are just as concerned about traffic and disruption that comes from high density real estate development as crime. Remember Steve Bartlett's oft repeated phrase in his first race, 'we don't need another real estate developer on the City Council.' "

"But everybody loves Ebby," I countered. She has a history of civic and political engagement. She's been in business for what seems like forever and is clearly the best known realtor in Dallas. Her home-for-sale signs are all over the city. And besides, Ebby's business is helping people buy and sell residential real estate. She's no developer and neither is Betty."

Skip continued. "Who do you think is supporting her? It's the real estate community, period. And besides, sure, everybody loves Ebby, but when they vote, her name won't be on the ballot. Look, it's only June and the election isn't until early March of next year. You have plenty of time to put a together a campaign and I believe you should consider the race. I hear she's ignoring Democrats. That's political naiveté. Old money is Democrat and more Democrats vote than Republicans in municipal elections. You'd have a certain populist appeal to them."

Paula, who had been listening from the kitchen, came in to enter the fray. "Skip, it only took Betty and Ebby a week to put together a steering committee. It includes all but one of the living past presidents of the North Dallas Chamber of Commerce. The one holdout is Jack Worley. Jim, doesn't Jack work at the same investment company you do?"

I reached out and hugged Paula for her empathy to my dilemma. "Yes, and I asked Jack why he wasn't supporting Betty. 'Because I know her' was his reply."

Bill had waited long enough to speak up. "That should tell you something. There must be a vulnerability that others would see."

He continued. "I know it's early but no one else has jumped in to challenge her. We're just now finding out about the open seat, but others have known about it for weeks. Most people knew that Joe only intended to serve two terms when he ran the first time."

Skip asked. "What's so important about the North Dallas Chamber of Commerce?"

I gave him Jack Worley's description. "It's the closest thing to an establishment for the business community of North Dallas. They are united behind Ebby." I cleared my throat and grinned, "I mean Betty." Jack Worley says that when they are united, they rarely, if ever, lose a local election." I stacked up all the arguments I'd told myself over the past week. "They have put together a juggernaut of a campaign and rumor has it that Ebby is raising a war chest of contributions to discourage others from joining the race."

Bill said, "I've heard that Jerry Bartos, a former member of the Dallas School Board, has been waiting for Joe Haggar to retire. Why doesn't he run? You know he wants to." Bill rose from his seat and answered his own question. "I'll tell you why. He shares the same political base as Betty and Betty has Ebby. Ebby could have supported Jerry but Betty moved first and she works for Ebby." He turned to me with good logic. "Jim, you have a different base of support. Your base would be younger people, people who have worked with you in Republican and city campaigns, Democrats, probably many neighborhood association members who are worried about zoning issues and traffic problems."

"Yes, I'm younger. When you went to the polling place to vote in the last election, any election, who was there waiting in line? Senior citizens! I remember the last time I voted I thought I was at a meeting of the Gray Panthers. Would they vote for a kid like me?"

"Only if you run." Skip threw his hands up.

"I've always pictured myself in the next ten or so years being in business with the ability to take time off from running my own business and to do politics as well." I looked toward the kitchen, curious as to the conversation in there. I expected Jetta to join us with her input. "But the timing isn't right for this one. I'm a corporate person now. If we need to issue securities or acquire another company it's all in 24-7. I'm not in a business that would allow me to do this on the side. And by the way, I love what I'm doing when we are in a frantic action mode, plus I've discovered I enjoy working on something larger than myself."

Skip's final pitch. "The reality is that opportunities rarely have perfect timing, or even good timing. Now is the opportunity, with the open seat. You have to grab it while it's there."

Liz leaned forward, "Jim, how are you taking all this personally? How does it feel to have this opportunity and the temptation to seize it?"

"I'm as excited as all git-out." *Sometimes my East Texas comes out of nowhere.* "I may be fantasizing but after two traditional terms at City Hall there could be other opportunities. I've always envied state senators, who seem to have more political power than those serving in the U.S. Congress, and that could be future step." *Now that would be exciting.* There's a real allure to a campaign. The intensity grows as Election Day approaches and you have less time to get your points across. Energy comes from speaking to a crowd and builds day by day. In a tight race it's a 24/7 adrenaline rush until it's over."

"THEN DO IT!" shouted Skip, Bill and Liz.

Of course, easy for them to say they're not giving up their jobs.

Paula came out of the kitchen to briefly listen to the discussion. When she slipped back behind the double doors, I wondered if it was to warn Jetta to put a stop to this wishful thinking. *Was it Paula's doubt or my own?*

My answer didn't encourage them. "Believe me, I want to and I don't care if the pay is fifty dollars a week. However, I know our company's CEO would never let me do this."

"If your employer won't back you, you can resign, borrow the money to live on for nine months if you need to and run." Bill said. "If you run and lose, you may end up in debt, but you'll find another full-time job. If you run and win, it should be easy to find an employer who will hire you and put up with your part time contribution for a few years in exchange for the prestige of having an elected official on their staff. At the cocktail parties they could brag, "You know that young kid on the City Council, he works for me. He's my boy."

Paula finally wrested Jetta from the kitchen. She stood just inside the room with one had on her hip and the other holding her wine glass. "Why would you quit the great job that you have and jump in front of Betty's steamroller of a campaign? Do you want to waste your time?" Jetta's questions came across as logical things that I was considering anyway. She wanted me to be practical.

One thing about being middle class and from a small town I wasn't afraid of going broke. I was broke when I came to Dallas and quickly got on my feet. I knew I could go broke and make it back again. I've been broke before; so broke I couldn't even pay attention and came back and believed I could do it again. But my larger worry was losing. I didn't want to lose my first and maybe only race.

"No," I said to the group, "It's not my time. The stakes are too high. I have a wife and young son, a mortgage and a six-figure job that I love and may not be able to replace."

Hearing that response, Jetta relaxed a little and poured herself another glass of wine. The tension that had been on her face seemed to slowly fade.

Those were my excuses for not doing it. The real reason was that I didn't have the confidence to believe the race was winnable. I know that now but didn't realize it then. I was resistant to change, as well. We sat down to lasagna and wine and I was back to my life of quiet desperation.

MY POLITICAL MENTOR

As June ended and July began, the heat outside became suffocating. The Texas weather was in that period when we were experiencing 100 plus degree days but were not used to it yet, as if we ever got used to the summer heat. I was still in a funk about letting myself back down and not taking advantage of the opportunity to run for an open seat. I was disappointed in myself. I was still intimidated and without the confidence to believe that I could run and win. A few of us in my political/social group did care about City Hall and wanted to be involved. We wondered if anyone else was going to run.

Why didn't someone else enter the race? Were all the potential candidates in the entire district intimidated by Betty and Ebby?

Those two were rapidly working the real estate industry and signing up commercial and residential real estate developers, bankers, brokers, attorneys, architects, and accountants, which, when the economy was booming seemed like about half the business community. As Dallas was a young, growing city, real estate development was a major industry. Dallas was one of the few cities in the United States, like New York, Chicago and Los Angeles where real estate was a profession. Several Dallas based firms had footprints around the country from their developments. All these named professionals were some of the folks who benefited in their own particular way by having a realtor or someone who favored real estate development on the City Council.

I had nothing against real estate development or growth; it just needed to be planned with adequate transportation facilities. One thing I learned quickly was when government makes important decisions there needs to be more than a simple majority in favor. Whether it's in Washington, state capitals, or on the local level at city halls, it's much better to have a consensus. You don't need unanimous support or approval, but the ultimate outcome has more chance of success and acceptance by citizens if there is a consensus. Many 6-5 decisions return for another round of debate while 11-0 or 10-1 or even 9-2 are settled once and for all. That's the importance of consensus and I believed I could be better at forging a deal on issues that could lead to a consensus than Betty could with her somewhat bombastic personality.

One of the questions of a rapidly growing city like Dallas involves land use regulations or zoning and the effect of development on transportation and mobility. Traffic was already a major problem in Dallas. Real estate development, both in Dallas and its encircling suburbs, created even more problems. The usual solution is more freeways to handle the traffic from suburbia. That solution fills the freeways with congestion from longer distance commuters. The tax base was growing in the suburbs where people were moving while transportation facility costs were largely borne by Dallas. In a city like Dallas encircled by suburbs, transportation was a regional issue. When cities like Dallas relax land use regulations and approve high density projects, whether near residential neighborhoods or not, communities can rebel. Resentment would manifest in the form of an angry citizenry voting "no" on bond elections, circulating petitions for tax rate rollbacks and recall elections for mayors and Council members. Growth has to be planned, supported by the citizens and supported by adequate transportation facilities. And the regional problems cried out for regional solutions.

Enid Gray, my friend from several campaigns was gaining a great reputation as a local political consultant. Enid's transition from volunteer to professional started with Steve Bartlett's populist campaign for the Dallas City Council and then increased with the Jack Evans campaign for mayor. As her reputation grew, she was also the consultant in several city bond elections, the campaign to approve DART (the rapid transit for Dallas and many surrounding cities), and the campaign to elect Steve Bartlett to Congress. Steve was preparing for a somewhat easy race in the general election after a bitter primary election battle. Enid had been instrumental in getting Steve elected with her targeting prowess. If the targeting is good, then money, volunteer and candidate time is used efficiently in phoning, mailers and walks.

The Bartlett campaign was fun, and I met a lot of folks who were deeply involved in politics. A few examples included Rex Jobe, a young technology entrepreneur who was one of Steve's finance chairmen, Jim Oberwetter, a public affairs executive for Hunt Oil Company, a major Dallas company, and Lisa La Master, a former journalist who became an expert in handling hostile media and served as Steve's media consultant. Lisa La Master had signed on as a campaign consultant/manager to Betty's campaign. Finally, I got to know Lisa Saeman, one of those "angels" who work tirelessly in a campaign. We recognized and respected each other's work ethic.

My brooding and second guessing were interrupted by a phone call one hot July day.

"Jim, it's Steve Bartlett." Before I could respond Steve launched into his reason for calling. "I have something for you to carefully consider. It looks like the only candidate in that District 3 Council race is going to be Betty Svoboda. She's rubbed a lot of people the wrong way, with her strong personality. We can't let her go unchallenged. There's no one in the race representing neighborhoods as a populist. That lane is wide open. You can beat her. I'm sure of it. You need to run!"

I was floored, even though Skip and Bill had tried to recruit me, I didn't think they were into Dallas politics enough to know whether I could win. Steve knew municipal politics, having just won re-election a couple of years before he ran for Congress. I never expected him to try to recruit me. Sure, we were allies and members of the same team, his team. I expected that Steve would be bogged down with the general election, but I guess the real battle was the primary.

"You really think I could win?" I asked.

"I know Dallas politics. You know I was involved in several campaigns before I ran and spent two terms at City Hall. I know you can win. You need to run."

"Then how will I win? What should I do?"

"The race is basically going to be single-family homeowners vs. the real estate developer community and taxpayers vs. the expanding bureaucracy of Chuck Anderson, the city manager."

"But Betty is a realtor, not a real estate developer and neither is Ebby."

"It doesn't matter. She still comes from that community. Remember my slogan 'We don't need another real estate developer on the City Council.' It worked when I ran against Pete Baldwin and won the at-large seat in a special election."

The realization that someone who knew what they were talking about and believed I could win made a huge difference in my attitude. I jumped on the possible opportunity immediately. That was all the encouragement I needed, except for one last detail. "May I use your name?"

"I can't formerly endorse you because of Ebby's contributions to my campaign and to the Republican Party. I just can't go against her with an endorsement like that."

"Well then can I say that you asked me to run? That should give you a partial excuse. In general it's never good to have only one unchallenged candidate in a race."

Steve hesitated, "I guess I can take the heat for that and use the lack of formal endorsement as an out. Call Enid and talk to her about it right away."

I called Enid as soon as that conversation was over. Someone other than me, who knew what they were talking about, wanted me to run. My emotional roller coaster continued. I had gone from mild depression (actually quiet desperation) to near euphoria in a 15-minute span of time. I suspected Enid was behind this and that Steve was the messenger. My suspicions were confirmed when the first thing she said was "Has Steve called you yet?"

"Yes. He said I could say he asked me to run. What do I do next?" Enid was the ultimate professional and municipal politics was her specialty. I was going to follow whatever plan she had in mind for me.

"First, ask your boss for permission to run. Make it soft, tell him

Steve ...no, Congressmen Steve Bartlett, asked you to run and see if he will agree to let you test the waters. Let him get used to the idea. If he says yes, I will give you a list of opinion leaders you need to call on, tell them you are considering the run and would like to see them and discuss it. Ask for their advice, not their support. They will remember that you came to them seeking their advice. If you run, they're more likely to support you. Betty isn't asking for anyone's advice. She's telling people what she's going to do and insisting they support her."

I knew the initial decision would first come from Bo West, my immediate supervisor. Bo and I went way back to my interview fifteen years ago with the CPA firm Deloitte Haskins & Sells while I was still in college, and he was still with the CPA firm. I remember him taking me to lunch at Cattlemen's Steakhouse in downtown Dallas. Ultimately, if Bo initially approved, then the final decision would come from our CEO and Chairman of the Board, E. Grant Fitts.

The next day I met with Bo. "Steve Bartlett asked me to run for City Council and I need your and Mr. Fitt's permission." Bo knew Steve.

"You know Fitts has the ultimate say. I'll approach him with it first, then you can ask him," was Bo's recommendation.

"Okay, but it's been recommended to me to just ask permission to test the waters."

"Well, that should make it easier."

I entered Mr. Fitts' office. He had a massive desk that he seemed to never use, choosing to sit on a couch at the other end of his office and work off a nearby coffee table. Grant Fitts looked like a lawyer and asked questions like a lawyer. He was a brilliant but somewhat eccentric attorney. Legend is that he grew up in an orphanage and went on to college to finish first in his class at Harvard and first in his class at Harvard Law School. He told us stories about commanding a transport ship during World War II and weathered storms hauling troops around Cape Horn from the Atlantic to the Pacific theatres.

He had gained control of a public company through some very strategic moves. No one knew exactly how old he was. He was rumored to have several different birth certificates with different birth years.

When I entered his office, he was asleep or pretending to be asleep sitting up. I knew better than to wake him. I sat down and waited. He woke up (or pretended to wake up) after a few minutes.

"So Jim, what's this I hear about the City Council? Don't you have enough work to do around here? I need to tell Bo to get you more involved."

I eyed the exit from his office in case I was told to leave. "Mr. Fitts, Congressman Steve Bartlett has asked me to run for the Dallas City Council, and I would like to test the waters and see if there is support for a race. I need your permission to do that."

After what seemed like thirty minutes of looking through a stack of papers on his desk, he looked up. "Why are you still here?'

Obviously, a test.

"I'm waiting on you to say yes."

To my surprise, he smiled. It was the first smile I had seen from him in the five years I had worked there. "Oh, all right. Get out of here and go see if you can drum up any support."

Any good salesman knows when you get the order; get out of the house/office/cafe, etc. before they change their mind.

"Thank you, Mr. Fitts," I quickly stepped out the door as he went back to reading his stack of papers.

Is this really happening? Now I might be able to be a candidate and keep my dream job. Is it true? Could it be true? A simple guy from a small town has an opportunity to take a major step.

I told Bo about Fitts' approval on the way back to my office and then called Enid. "I'm in, at least for the first phase."

"Great. Come by tomorrow afternoon and I'll have a list of people for you to go see. Some will have already agreed to endorse Betty but that doesn't mean they can't talk you up a little bit." Enid raised her voice. "And remember, tell them that you're considering the race and value their advice."

I spent the rest of the afternoon alone in my office putting together a preliminary political resume. It was hard to concentrate because I was so excited. When I got home I was ready to celebrate. I walked through the door and announced the evening's plans to Jetta by breaking out into song. "Put on your red dress baby, cause we're going out tonight." I didn't sound anything like Carl Perkins.

Jetta was in the living room reading and the smile on her face revealed relief by the shift in my mood, which had been fairly dark lately.

"What's that all about?" she asked. "You haven't been in this good of a mood since you were offered a job at Gulf."

"Gee, you must have missed the good mood I had a few years back," I laughed. "I get to keep my job and run for the Council, or at least I have permission to test the waters. Mr. Fitts gave me a tentative okay," I replied. "Let's have a family night."

She smiled. "Well good, you get to keep your job after all. That's the most important thing."

I wouldn't have expected any other response from her. And she was right. Jetta, our two-year-old son, Murk, and I went out for a celebratory dinner.

TESTING THE WATERS

It was August, the first week after I had obtained permission from Mr. Fitts, to at least test the waters for the upcoming election. My life was about to change as I would be spending more time selling myself to opinion leaders and less time working with attorneys, accountants and investment analysts about our company's various business interests. It would be a new activity for me. I was completely committed to my new circumstances.

Enid had given me explicit instructions about how to talk to the opinion leaders. "Give them a short pitch about who you are and why you are considering the race." I had always been able to follow simple instructions from professionals.

Enid and I sat in the conference room at her office. The conference room had a TV with split screens so one could watch more than one news cast. There were photographs on the walls of office holders she had helped get elected, first as a volunteer and later as a professional political consultant. Her advice was highly sought by candidates and high officials at many levels of government. There were newspaper clippings scattered about on the conference table to remind everyone of local news events that might impact an election.

Enid leaned back in her chair and took in a deep breath. "These are people who may not necessarily be powerful, although some are, and they may not necessarily be rich, although some are. These are people who care deeply about Dallas and spend a lot of time supporting efforts to help it grow and prosper. They are more concerned about the City's well-being than having anything to gain from a particular project or development. Their friends, acquaintances and co-workers look to them for advice on who are the best candidates to support."

She leaned forward toward me. "Now go meet with them and put your charm to work. Make sure you separate yourself from your opponent, Betty. Stress how you are different without criticizing her. Be confident but humble."

I stood up, eager to get started. I fidgeted from one foot to the other like a little boy waiting to be dismissed before going out to play with his friends. "Thanks for the advice. I'm looking forward to the meetings and will begin setting them up at once."

A typical meeting would be in an office at a business or non-profit and would include a conversation much like this. "Hello, I'm Jim Richards. I've been asked to run for Dallas City Council in District 3." I would tell them about my family, what I did for a living, what city boards I had served on and about my volunteer work in the last bond election. I also mentioned that I was presently on the Dallas Civil Service Board and board of directors of the Wayback House and the Women's Wayback House, two halfway houses for folks leaving prison and on parole. The Women's House was a project of the Wayback House and I spent a lot of time there setting up the books. I would end with a joke. "I'll only run if Tom Landry doesn't," knowing that the popular coach of the Cowboys could easily win if he ran, but wouldn't have any interest in something like this.

Concluding my pitch or inquiry I asked if they had any interest in the race for themselves or had another candidate in mind. Then I would ask for their advice. Overall the feedback was good, given a sprinkling of bad news. "Ebby has already been by and it's really hard to say no to her. I had to commit to Ebby that I would support Betty."

These were opinion leaders and when folks asked them about the race, even if they said they were supporting Betty, I wanted them in good conscience to say, "...but I met the other guy and he seems perfectly alright with me."

However, most of the opinion leaders I met with stated something like, "I'm glad to hear that she might have competition. A candidate who runs unopposed usually ends up overly confident and not as good a listener to citizens. A race against a strong opponent always informs and cautions a candidate to listen to what people are saying. Good luck to you, young man."

Some of the opinion leaders were uncommitted; perhaps I had reached them before Ebby or Betty. "I'll seriously consider you if you decide to run and I hope you will pursue the race." Others gave a hedged promise, "I'll say now that I'll support you if you run against Betty, but I must include a caveat that I can't if one of my good friends runs, which at this late date is highly unlikely."

The list also included several folks rumored to be considering the race. One was Wayne Calloway, who ran Frito Lay for PepsiCo. I called Mr. Calloway's office for a meeting.

When he finally consented to the meeting, I went to the Frito Lay Tower in Exchange Park, a mixed-use development near Love Field, the City's urban airport. Since Wayne Calloway was not only a potential candidate and the CEO of a major Dallas company, this meeting was important. I rehearsed my words several times on my way to his office. It was late afternoon and most of the employees had left work. I found his office. The door was open. It was a large private office, decorated as one would expect a CEO's office should be. Nice and neat but not ostentatious. Very business-like with evidence of their brands in strategic places.

I opened with "Mr. Calloway, I'm Jim Richards and I believe we have an appointment this afternoon." I cleared my throat and began to worry about what I was going to say or do if he said he had decided to run himself.

"Yes, please come in and have a seat. My secretary had to leave early but can I get you anything?" he offered.

"No but thank you for the offer," I responded, thinking how nice this guy is.

"I'm really glad to meet you and have the opportunity to discuss the City of Dallas. Since Joe Haggar is retiring, I'm considering running for the seat he holds on the City Council and I understand you're considering the race as well, or at least several folks are trying to talk you into running." There was a sinking feeling in the pit of my stomach as I continued. "I'd appreciate knowing whether you're seriously considering the race and your views on city issues. We need more business people, other than real estate developers in City government."

He interrupted to agree with that, at least with the need for more business people. "Yes, we do." Wayne Calloway was known for listening more than talking. He had a reputation for intuitive insight into people.

I continued, "I'm a business executive but frankly don't have your stature. In politics I've been more of a grass roots organizer than a fund raiser. Hell, I may want to support you if you run."

Wayne's reply was what I would have expected from an executive of his caliber. "Oh, I do care a lot about the City, but I've got plenty to do here at Frito Lay. We're rapidly expanding and my plate is full right now." While someone like him might run for mayor after retirement, his corporate job was probably more challenging and appealing to him than being one of ten members of the Dallas City Council.

"Well, if you make a final decision not to run, I would appreciate your support for me if I run. Thank you very much for the meeting. I do appreciate your time and counsel."

"Certainly, I'm glad you came by and glad to see more action in the race, assuming you decide to run. Good luck!"

Wayne Calloway left Frito Lay the next year to move up to eventually be president of its Parent Company, PepsiCo and to serve as an independent director on the boards of Exxon Mobil, Citicorp and General Electric. Here was an example of the changing nature of the Dallas business community. Instead of a company founder being available to leave their business part time to serve, the CEO's of today were managing multinational corporations that needed their full-time attention. Wayne was a perfect example of someone the downtown business community, the Dallas Citizens Council, would love to have at City Hall. In the unlikely event that someone of his stature would run, he would have overwhelming support from those business leaders. He had much more responsibility at PepsiCo so that opened the door for a young activist like me to run.

Which is better, in the abstract? A business leader who would most likely make decisions based on what they thought would be good for the City as a whole over what their single-member district citizens wanted or someone who might be more politically adept and understand that voters' attitudes matter when it comes to approval of capital projects in bond elections.

The general obligation bonds used to finance projects must be approved by the voters, not just the City Council. When voters get angry about government's actions, about not being heard, they vote against bond elections. When voters get angry, demigods are more likely to be elected to public office. Single-member districts allow more folks with lower profiles, more young people and more political activists, who may be more adept at listening to voters than civic leaders, to get involved and win elections. Self-government needs citizen involvement, old and young, men and women.

AN INSURMOUNTABLE OBSTACLE

Fall was here as September turned to October and leaves began to turn from green to orange and red. The first day a chill was in the air. The State Fair of Texas was going strong and football seasoned had started. The season was turning and so was my confidence. I became more optimistic about chances of running and winning. I was really feeling like a candidate and enjoying it. I was looking forward to the campaign.

Early October meant that I would need to get a final answer from our CEO, Mr. Fitts, as to whether I had permission to run. Based on our previous meeting, I fully expected his approval. I cleared everything with Bo and made an appointment to meet with Mr. Fitts again to get what I thought would be the go-ahead. He had given me permission to test the waters and see what kind of support I would have, which turned out to be strong among City-wide opinion leaders, despite the groundwork that Ebby had laid out for Betty. There were a lot of uncommitted folks out there because Ebby couldn't meet or talk to all the opinion leaders' one on one and some of them already knew Betty.

I was taking a risk just asking if I could run because that could put me in the category of someone who wasn't committed to the company. I knew if I ran and lost, I would be embarrassed and humiliated. I thought the reward was so large that I gave little, if any, consideration to the risk. My attitude by that time had become "Damn the torpedoes, full speed ahead."

At the appropriate time I practically stormed into Fitts' office brimming with confidence. Like always, he was sitting on the couch in his office, using the coffee table as a desk. He was leaning back on the couch with his feet propped up on the coffee table, looking relaxed. He looked up. He didn't say anything but just looked at me with an icy stare. I was taken aback but tried not to show it. It was a cold and dreary day outside. Maybe the gray sky was an omen.

"Mr. Fitts, I've made the rounds and the feedback from the opinion leaders was quite good. I'm ready to run and would appreciate your blessing. I can assure you that I will get my work done here. I'm used to working 60 to 70-hour weeks and that is enough time to cover both. I'll have to campaign 24-7 for a few months but after that I will be available 50 hours a week to get my work done here. How about it?"

This time there were no faked distractions, no teasing like our previous meeting when he endorsed my testing the waters. He stiffened and shook his head. Then he sternly said, "No, you can't do it. It wouldn't look good to the board and the shareholders. You need to be devoted to one or the other and you must choose now. This is final. I'm sorry but there will be no discussion, argument or debate about this."

I felt an immediate flush in my face and stepped back. "But!" was all I could get out before he continued.

"No buts. It's your choice. You can run, or you can work here."

What a punch in the gut. All the joy, the hope, I had experienced the last few months left me. I couldn't bring myself to say anything. Knowing him, this wasn't a joke. I knew this was final and non-debatable. I felt humiliated.

With a wife and a two-year-old son, I had no choice but to stay with the company. I tried to soften the blow by reminding myself how much I loved my work here. I left his office without saying another word, but singing to myself the chorus from the hauntingly beautiful theme song from M*A*S*H.

Suicide is painless it brings on many changes and I can take or leave it if I please.

I wasn't seriously thinking of suicide, but these words captured the despair I was feeling at the time but didn't dare show it to anyone at the company.

The job at Gulf United was a dream job for a guy like me. I had spent ten years at the CPA firm of Deliotte Haskins & Sells, now part of Deliotte Touche and had two of the most interesting clients. One of my major clients was SEDCO, Inc., an international oil drilling contractor, the CEO of which was Bill Clements, who later became the governor of Texas. I had traveled to Iran twice to work for them and also had an assignment in Singapore. The other major client was Gulf United, the company for which I had left Deliotte Haskins & Sells. Gulf United was what was called a "Holding Company." In fact, the first name of the Company was Gulf Life Holding Company. I was part of a small corporate staff at headquarters and we had subsidiaries in several industries, notably life insurance, radio television broadcasting and real estate, although our real estate holdings were primarily far to the north of the City of Dallas. I had diverse duties, examination of potential acquisition targets, coordination with the outside auditors, installing and coordinating a corporate planning and reporting system, filings with the Securities and Exchange Commission and investor relations and dealing with stock analysts. We had a corporate jet and an apartment in mid-town Manhattan. It was a heady experience for a kid like me, but I knew it was coming to a close in the near future because the investment bank Lehmann Brothers, had begun exploring for potential buyers of our life insurance sector companies.

The rest of the afternoon I sat bewildered, alone in my office with the door closed. It took me over an hour to pull myself together and try to come to grips with the abrupt reversal of Fitts's position. What changed? My dream of running had turned into a nightmare. My sadness eventually turned to a mild anger as I began imagining what probably happened.

Maybe he thought of it as kind of a joke, that I really wouldn't get any support and it was just a lark to let me test the waters. Maybe he thought I would see that no support was available and forget about the race. Maybe he thought I couldn't win and believed a loss would put him and the company in a bad light. Maybe someone got to him or got to somebody on the board. He did mention that my running wouldn't look good to the board. Who could it have been? Was I that big of a threat to someone? These questions haunted me for a long time. Thirty-five years later I still don't know what really happened.

As I pondered these questions, I looked around my office since it looked like I would be there for a while, at least until the company sold. It was really nice. It had been Eddie Acker's office during his time at Gulf United. Eddie was a former executive with Braniff Airways and came to Gulf with the title of president. He and Grant were both too headstrong to share authority, so his tenure was brief. He soon left to take a job as CEO of another airline, Air Florida and later Pan Am. His three contributions were to acquire an apartment in Manhattan, acquire a corporate jet and recommend that the Company hire someone for strategic planning, which turned out to be me. The furniture in my office came from Eddie's office at Braniff. The couch reflected Braniff's colors and the paint patterns of planes, a mixture of bright reds, oranges and greens. When our company was in an acquisition fight or registering securities to take advantage of market conditions some of us stayed at the office all night for a few days in a row. It was nice to have a place like the Braniff couch to catch a half hour sleep before morning came.

I called Enid with the news. "Fitts said no and the no was final, so I'm out." Enid was professional about the bad news. She must have anticipated that something like this could happen and already had a Plan B ready. What she said next added to the mystery and gave me the feeling someone, somewhere was pulling the strings.

"Mayor Jack Evans isn't running for re-election." Jack was the former CEO of Cullum Companies, the parent of the giant Tom Thumb grocery chain. "The Cullum family called Jack back to work. There were problems that they thought only he could solve so they asked him to return as the CEO." Jack was a member of what some of us light heartedly called the Bent Tree Mafia, a group of men who lived in the Bent Tree neighborhood of Far North Dallas and seemed to have a disproportional amount of influence in the City.

Enid went on. "Stark Taylor, the current president of the Park Board is running for mayor and needs your help. His opponent will be former Mayor Wes Wise, who will run a populist campaign. I'm Taylor's campaign consultant. He'll be able to raise plenty of money but has zero political experience and no connection to the grass roots. Now that you're not running you need to get involved in his campaign."

"Well, I might as well do something. What?"

"Host a party at your home and invite all the Republican grass roots activists that you know to meet him. Introduce him, pledge your support and strongly recommend that they seriously consider him. Then go to work and help build a bipartisan, city wide precinct organization. Something good should result from you doing this. But first there is an unpleasant task. Call everyone back that you visited with and tell them you're not running. Don't volunteer the reason. If you are pressed, use the same excuse everybody uses. Tell them you need to spend more time with your family."

Having accepted Mr. Fitt's verdict that I couldn't run for office while an officer of our company, I chose to call off the campaign, rather than risk resigning and running without a job. Had I run and won, it would have been easier to find work but if I had lost it would have been much harder. *Who wants to hire a loser?* As Bill and Skip suggested, I could have borrowed enough to pay my bills during the next five months but what about after that, especially if I didn't win. I agonized over this question.

Am I using the lack of a secure job as an excuse? I've had a secure job for fifteen years and have always been able to find work. As a teenager at the grocery store, at the gas station and in the oil patch in East Texas and later after finishing college and moving to Dallas with Deloitte Haskins & Sells and Gulf United. Jobs seemed to have sought me out and I have been working for as long as I can remember. Was I afraid I would not be able to find a job? No! Was I really afraid to go up against Betty and Ebby, lose and not have a job? Probably!

I spent the next two months telling my close friends and family that Fitts wouldn't let me run after all. It was about the same conversation with each friend I spoke to. "I'm not running. Fitts decided not to let me keep my job and run to serve in office, even though the feedback was positive." I felt like a teenager telling my friends I can't join them because my parents won't let me.

The next emotionally difficult step was calling back all of the opinion leaders and telling them the campaign was off. As fun and exhilarating the calls were before Fitts changed his mind, the call backs were demoralizing. Not something I wanted to do but something Enid, my campaign consultant, advised.

Some of the opinion leaders didn't have much of a response, others said they were disappointed and hoped I would try again down the line and most wished me luck. All appreciated the call. The call backs were necessary, and Enid was right in telling me to do it. People who are this involved in civic and government affairs appreciated a personal call, rather than hearing it from somebody else or reading about it in the newspaper.

In my despair I thought back to the time I met Sid Stahl a few months ago. Sid, a prominent opinion leader was a Dallas attorney who was serving at-large on the Council and was not running for re-election. I had gone to see Sid in his law office at Geary Stahl and Spencer in downtown Dallas.

Sid was one of those guys who didn't stoke his ego by sitting behind an oversized desk. He did a great job on the City Council, he was an excellent attorney and a rainmaker for his firm. Yet, he was humble and came around his desk to sit beside me. I thought this is the kind of guy I want to be when someone asks me for advice. As we sat facing each other Sid said something that I will never forget: "You know Jim, the important thing to remember is that one person can make a difference."

It was inspirational. I kept remembering that piece of advice and it made me want to run and serve my city and state even more. I could have been part of something larger than myself. I could do something worthwhile. The guy from small town East Texas could have helped the City. One person can make a difference.

RESURRECTION

I had reconciled that I wouldn't be running for the City Council but would continue to be politically active. I decided to take Enid's advice and jump into the Taylor for Mayor Campaign. Starke was the son of a cotton broker who took over and ran his family's business until the time was right to sell it to a firm from Switzerland who did the same thing on a larger scale. Starke had been president of the Dallas Park Board, the most prestigious and coveted board or commission that the City Council appoints.

The Park Board had near absolute authority over all the park and recreation facilities of the city, including numerous recreation centers, swimming pools, golf courses, tennis courts, and special facilities like Fair Park; home of the State Fair of Texas, the Dallas Zoo and eventually, the Dallas Arboretum and Botanical Gardens. Starke got to know Betty Svoboda, who was also on the Park Board when both of them served together. That experience of working together would play an important role involving me a few months later.

So now the first task was helping introduce Starke to the political activist community. He knew many of the CEO's in the area and most of the potential money raisers and donors but not many of the grass roots leaders. That was where I could help, having toiled in many Republican and non-partisan campaigns and served in three different officer positions of the Republican Men's Club.

I don't know who invented the neighborhood coffee concept, but many campaigns use it. A host couple invites neighborhood residents, within a few square miles of where they live, over for coffee and light desserts and to meet the candidate. The event could be on a Saturday during the day, a Sunday afternoon or weekday evening. It's a come and go, meet the candidate in person and ask any questions you like. At the end, the candidate gives a short speech, and then says goodbye and leaves. I decided on a version of that concept to introduce Starke to the activists I could round up.

After telling Jetta about Enid's request that we give a party, I ran a new idea past her. "In addition to coffee and soft drinks, let's serve hors d'oeuvres, along with beer and wine. Let's turn the neighborhood coffee into a real party."

Jetta was excited and didn't want to be left out. "I'll start planning the food and drinks and hire someone to help serve and clean up."

Working with Enid and Starke's scheduler, we picked a week day evening thinking that a weekend would be less attended. The date was within the next two weeks. Time was short, and we had a party to give. I telephoned every active Republican I knew, concentrating on precinct chairs, organizers, and club officers so as to focus on the opinion leaders of the grass roots. What Starke needed and what I could provide, was introduction to the grass roots leaders who could help recruit the workers.

"I want to invite you to a function to introduce you to the next mayor of the City of Dallas, Starke Taylor," was how every telephone conversation started. Although no one said it, I knew that many of the more conservative activists didn't trust Starke, thinking he was a closet moderate, which he was. I was never a true believer in conservative politics and many of those folks didn't trust that I was conservative enough either, but they did respect my work for various candidates and this was my candidate. I didn't pick candidates because of their conservative ideology. I tried to help good people get elected and believed Starke was one of those good people that make for good government.

In addition to the phone calls there was food, beer and wine to buy and a server to hire. Since I was working at the time, most of those functions fell upon Jetta. By the night of the party, the house was immaculate. The bar was open and everything was going as planned.

The first guest arrived about 6:45 p.m. and then a flood of people poured in between 7:00 and 7:15. I greeted our guests at the door with words like, "So glad you could come by, come in and help yourself. The candidate will be here soon." People ate, drank and mingled with each other, looking around and discussing among themselves just who had turned out and who wasn't there.

Enid came in around 7:25 and huddled with Jetta and I. "Starke will be here any minute. Wow, what a crowd and your home looks great."

"Jetta gets credit. She did all the work, prepared the food and picked up the drinks."

Jetta smiled. "Jim raised the crowd. I hope the candidate gets here soon, because people are getting antsy."

Enid replied "Let them anticipate. It will provide some excitement when he arrives."

Finally, Starke's driver dropped him and a member of his campaign staff off and left to find a parking place. I greeted him at the door in the entry way. "Hi Starke, I'm Jim Richards."

"I know who you are. Thanks for the party."

"Ladies and Gentlemen, our candidate for mayor of Dallas, Starke Taylor." I announced his arrival over a din of conversation. He started meeting people and shaking hands. His manager led him around the room and introduced folks who didn't introduce themselves. People had been showing up all along. By that time it was a little crowded downstairs and that was desirable. No one wants to give a party like this in a semi-empty house.

Unlike many houses today with open floor plans, our house was older and had separate living and dining rooms joined by the entryway and staircase. The dining room was behind the kitchen and behind the kitchen was a large rectangle den. People were wall-to-wall in the living and dining rooms. The crowd overflowed into an adjoining bedroom. Some folks in the den, located behind the kitchen had positioned themselves at the bar, perhaps not wanting to be any closer which might show a sign of commitment.

By about 8:00 Enid knew the time was right. "Call everybody to come within hearing distance and introduce the candidate." I called everyone to come closer to where we were. We stood in front of the fireplace at one end of the living room for the introduction and his speech.

I had to raise my voice over the buzz of many conversations. "Okay; it's time for the candidate to speak. Please come as close as you can."

"I'm Jim Richards and I want to thank you all for coming." Even though everyone knew me, I had been around politics long enough to develop the habit of repeating my name when I could. "I want to introduce a good friend of mine. He's a businessman, who ran a wholesale cotton business for a number of years. We need more men and women from the business world in political office. He's been active in civic affairs and City government as the immediate past president of the Dallas Park Board, which makes him practically the mayor already," I joked. A few got it or at least humored me with a half laugh when I laughed. "He's been a strong contributor and supporter of Republican candidates and is an admirable conservative. Please help me in welcoming the next mayor of the City of Dallas, Starke Taylor."

I clapped loudly, hoping everyone else would too. They did. I shook his hand and stepped aside. It was a thrill to have that many grass roots leaders turnout. I have always drawn energy and enthusiasm from a crowd of people and this was a crowd I had turned out and hosted. It was a good moment, but it didn't last long.

When the applause died down, the room got quiet, awfully quiet as if the crowd was waiting on the candidate to give a stem-winding oration. It got even quieter as he stood there saying nothing.

Finally, he read (stammered) through his canned speech, obviously written by a consultant and not really what he thought, much less felt. At times he turned to his manager to explain the things he couldn't. As I looked over the audience I could see folks frowning and glancing at each other. I faked a smile and shifted my weight from one foot to the other, back and forth.

Starke finally spoke of himself and said, "My forte is dealing with people, creating relationships, which is sorely needed. I applied that skill in the cotton business, raising money for political candidates and while serving on the Park Board."

Yes! Now, finally, that's more like it. People want to hear you talk about who you are and what you believe. So, now he's real. Now he sounds authentic.

When he finished I stood up and clapped energetically and the crowd followed, although not nearly as enthusiastic as before. "Thanks to everybody for coming and thanks to Starke for telling us about himself and what he wants to accomplish."

Starke followed with "Yes, thank you all for coming and thanks to the Richards for hosting this event." With that he and his handler left for the night.

After the crowd left and with only a few of our closest friends remaining, I turned to Enid. "I like Starke a lot, I know he's a good guy and will be a good mayor, but it may be a long row to hoe to get him elected."

"That's why you have to get involved. Let's get together tomorrow and talk about what else you can do. And remember, Jim, he's never done anything close to this before. Cut him some slack."

"Of course, I'll get involved. I like Starke, he's qualified and will make a great mayor."

During November and December, I toiled in the weeds for the Taylor for Mayor Campaign, helping with the phone center and building a City-wide precinct organization. The precinct organization was usually led by regional captains and precinct captains, which had to be recruited. The precinct organization was used for walks for the candidate and recruitment of volunteers within each precinct.

The phone center was for voter ID (identification of prospective voters for the candidate). We called and identified those supporting the candidate, who was against and who was undecided. The folks against the candidate were left alone, the undecided were sent a mailer and called back later. We saved the names of those for the candidate, whether in the first round or later, for GOTV (Get Out The Vote). We called them back on election day to tell them where they are supposed to vote and kept calling them until they said they had voted or until the polls closed.

These were both traditional grass roots activities. In addition, there were other functions for those volunteers who didn't like to talk to strangers on the phone but liked to be at headquarters, working with others to fold and stuff brochures into envelopes to be mailed to undecided voters.

I kept busy with the Taylor campaign. The work there fueled my desire to do something more. I was the previous chair of the Ushering and Greeting Committee of my church, Preston Hollow Methodist, and was presently serving on the City of Dallas Civil Service Board and the boards of the two half way houses. Despite all these activities, I still felt like something greater was never going to happen to me and I was back to my life of quiet desperation, although slightly adjusted upward to mildly active desperation.

Being involved in politics can be addicting. The more you achieve, the more you want to do and the more yen you have to do something bigger.

The filing deadline for the March elections was a few weeks away and no one had filed to challenge Betty Svoboda. That bothered a lot of people who were not enamored with the prospect of a Councilwoman Svoboda, including Starke Taylor, whose race for mayor looked optimistic.

The longer she went without an opponent, the more she exuded the hubris she was known for. As the date for the deadline for filing came closer, the more confident of winning she became. Potential candidates were intimidated by her (and Ebby) and she knew it. No one was going to challenge her, and she was getting bolder each day. I still wanted to run and would pace the floor at night, going over the events of the past few months again and again. I always reached the same conclusion. I couldn't run. After my nightly routine of hashing this out I would finally throw up my hands in an "I give up" gesture to myself and fell into a restless night's sleep.

December came and went and now it was early January. The

Dallas Cowboys were in the playoffs after a 6 and 3 strike-shortened, nine game regular season and faced the Tampa Bay Buccaneers in the first round on January 9, 1983. I watched the game by myself in the den at the back of our house that Sunday and enjoyed the 30 to 17 victory. When the Boys win, a good mood seems to engulf the North Texas area. Bars and restaurants have their best nights after a Cowboy victory. For some reason, a victory seemed to be an omen for change and change for me was about to come.

About 8:30 p.m. the phone rang with news that blew me away. It was Bo West, my boss at Gulf United. His message was short and sweet. "Jim, get ready for a campaign. It's almost certain, and I will confirm it in the morning."

"What happened? I thought the answer was an emphatic no."

"At halftime of the Cowboy game today, our box at Texas Stadium was visited by a delegation representing Starke Taylor. The gentlemen wanted to talk to Grant Fitts. Our box was full so we stepped out into the hall."

It was starting to sink in that this could be real. "A delegation? Who was included?"

Bo replied. "Joe Haggar, Grant's next-door neighbor and the existing Council member from Northwest Dallas and Vance Jobe."

Vance was a member of the "Bent Tree Mafia" that was strongly behind Starke. In addition to Starke, two immediate former mayors, Robert Folsom and Jack Evans, came from the Bent Tree neighborhood that Mayor Folsom's company had developed.

"I know Vance Jobe, his son Rex is a friend of mine who I worked with in the Bartlett campaigns. Everyone knows Joe Haggar."

Bo continued, repeating what they said to Grant and anyone else in the hallway. "Joe Haggar took the lead. He said he wasn't running for re-election and that Starke Taylor wants Jim to be able to run for the Council against Betty Svoboda. He also emphasized that because the election is in early March, there's only two months left to campaign. Finally, he said that they understand Jim needs your permission to run while still in your employ and that both they and Starke would appreciate it if he would give it." Grant then said, "Sure, that's OK by me."

The whole conversation took about 90 seconds and that gave me a glimpse into just how much some people in town can accomplish by having the stature of a man like Joe Haggar. I doubt that Fitts knew who Starke Taylor was, but he knew his neighbor Joe Haggar and knew he was a respected pillar of the community and the Catholic Church and its educational institutions in the Dallas area.

"You better get ready to run because the election is less than two months away. I'll get a confirmation tomorrow and let you know."

"I'll be in the office before you get there."

I ran through the house calling out, looking for Jetta. I grabbed her and shared the unbelievably good news. "Wow" was all she could say.

We were in shock, but it was a great shock. A natural high, an excitement. I couldn't conceive of being more excited than when I heard the news that night. My life was about to undergo a radical change, from being on the sidelines watching to being in the game. As we say in sports, "We're going to the dance." Someone was going to challenge Betty after all and it was going to be me.

Jetta was relieved that finally I was going to get to run, stop brooding about it, and not give up my job, at least not at first. I told her, "This is going to be a major undertaking, and I won't get to see you and Murk much for the two months of the campaign. I hope you'll help and tolerate my absence."

"I'm just glad you won't be giving up the paycheck. Go and work hard at this and beat Betty. Murk and I will be here when it's over."

"When I win, I'll reserve Wednesday nights after the Wednesday afternoon Council meetings for family night and Sundays for "buddy days" to spend all day with Murk."

The comfort that Jetta and I felt by my keeping my job while I ran was somewhat overstated. The 1980's were a time of acquisitions and takeovers, many of which were hostile, opposed by the company being acquired. Since I started at Gulf United, the company had acquired two life insurance companies, a pharmaceutical distribution company, three broadcast companies (each with a television station and both AM and FM radio), and another large radio group with multiple stations.

While we had numerous defenses against a hostile takeover, Mr. Fitts had always said that anything and everything we had was for sale at the right price. We all knew a sale of either our entire company or various pieces would eventually come, and we would be out of a job. In fact, discussions with various groups had already started. We knew the end wasn't far away. Nevertheless, I was focused on the immediate upcoming campaign and didn't have time to think about the longer time frame of selling out in the next year or so.

Of course, the first phone call I made that evening was to Enid. I was brimming with excitement when I called to tell her about the conversation.

I got a simple "Okay that's great. Call me at the Weekly Gray McKinney world headquarters tomorrow after you get confirmation and let's get started." Enid's partner was John Weekly and the office was on McKinney Avenue, hence the name, Weekly Gray McKinney. "I'm not allowed to run your campaign, but I have a proxy in mind that will be ready to help."

It's like she knew this was going to happen. I wondered if Enid orchestrated this coup behind the scenes. Needless to say, I didn't get or want much sleep that night but a mini-celebration was in order, even though by that time it was late on a Sunday night. I opened a beer and re-watched M*A*S*H, one of my favorite movies on TV late, into the night.

BUILDING A CAMPAIGN STRUCTURE

Eight Weeks Till Election Day

The next morning, I got confirmation that yes, I could run. I called Enid to let her know and then started to work. I started to build my campaign by calling my immediate friends with the news.

Dan and Teddie Garrigan were good friends of both Jetta and I. Teddie and Jetta had worked together as volunteers at an organization for rape victims called the Rape Crises Center. They even ran the organization at one time. Dan met both Jetta and Teddie in his capacity as a prosecutor for Henry Wade, the famous district attorney of Dallas County. We had taken a joint vacation to New England with the Garrigans in August when it looked like I might get to run before Mr. Fitts changed his mind. The four of us celebrated my opportunity to run by going to dinner together at the University Club, where I still had a company membership. We enjoyed good food and talked about City politics and the campaign. It was my last "meal" for the next two months, other than whatever was served at campaign events or a late-night hamburger take-out at the Jack-in-the-Box to eat with a beer at home after a day of constant campaigning.

I told Bill Booher the news the first day. His response was positive. "I'll do whatever needs to be done. I know I helped talk you into this so what can I do?"

I jumped on that. "I need a campaign treasurer if you're willing to take on that responsibility."

"I said anything. So, what is the responsibility of the campaign treasurer?" he asked.

"I did that for Bartlett in one of his City races. You'll deposit all the contribution checks, write all the expense checks and file the campaign finance reports with the City secretary. In addition to that, I want to use your experience as advice for strategy."

"You bet. The strategy will be fun." Bill ended up being an essential part of the campaign and a long-time friend.

I knew money was going to be important, having worked on it in the Bartlett campaign. The only fund raiser I knew was Rex Jobe, who had been one of Bartlett's finance chairs. I visited with Rex in his home in the Preston Hollow neighborhood in North Dallas.

After telling Rex the story of the campaign being on, then off, then on again I made a request. "Rex, I knew you were involved with finance in Bartlett's campaign and now I need help myself. I've asked a few folks for support and left a donation card with them. Some money has come in but not much. Can you help me as my finance chair?"

"Jim, I'm really involved in my business right now, but I still want to help. I want you to win and will make phone calls but that's about all I can do for the next few months, which is when you're going to need help. I wish it were different, but I will do as much as I can."

"Any help will be appreciated, Rex. I know you're busy and I'm glad your business is doing well." We wished each other good luck and I left. Anything he can raise will be helpful.

The next day I asked Enid. "Who can advise me on the issues? Who can give me a big picture overview?"

"You need to talk to Phil Seib." Phil was the local public affairs columnist with the *Dallas Morning News*. "He's a good friend of mine so call him for an appointment."

"Good. I don't know Phil, but I read his column."

I called that afternoon. "Hi Phil, this is Jim Richards. I'm a friend of Enid Gray and am running for the Dallas City Council. Enid says I need to talk to you. Can I see you sometime soon for a cup of coffee?"

We met a few days later at the coffee shop in one of the hotels along Central Expressway. After a few pleasantries, Phil said "Okay, Jim. So, you're running for City Council. What do you need from me?

How can I help you?"

I gave Phil my standard introductory pitch about my profession, my civic work and involvement in city elections, boards and commissions. "When I'm elected, I want to be an energetic advocate for improved transportation infrastructure and will campaign hard for DART. I'm in a tough race and I got a late start. I'd appreciate any advice you could spare for me. What can I do in your opinion? What does this district, what does Dallas need and what are people asking about? What are their concerns?"

Phil's role at the *Dallas Morning News* gave him an excellent grounding in the City and its politics. He was direct. "The economy is this area is booming, especially in the northern part of the City, which includes over half of Dallas. There is strong demand here for real estate development. Practically all over the City, real estate developers are seeking to up-zone properties that they have acquired or have an option to acquire, pending a change in zoning. That means more density, height, or change in use that makes the property more valuable. It also has a tendency to decrease the value of the surrounding single-family properties and increase the traffic problems in those neighborhoods."

"Sounds like it will be an issue in every race," I said.

"It's becoming a real political issue, even a city-wide issue. It may not be in every race, but it certainly is in the Oak Lawn area, East Dallas, North Dallas and Far North Dallas. The streets are crowded, and traffic is becoming as congested as Houston traffic, where they don't have any zoning restrictions. Candidates who recognize this and take a stand are going to emerge very well. People are listening to candidates to understand their position on this issue. They're looking for authenticity. That's the advice I would give any candidate who asks and your opponent hasn't asked."

Well who wondered why, her being backed by the real estate community and the North Dallas Chamber of Commerce, besides not really receptive of advice? For me, this was damn good advice. Plus, it never hurts to have friends with organizations that buy ink by the boxcar load.

"Thank you, Phil. My positions have been somewhat fluid at first but they are firming up. While I don't have a history as a neighborhood activist, I'm developing a good feel for what's important to neighborhoods all over the City. Anything I can do for you?"

"No, but good luck and tell Enid I said hello."

The next stop was going to be with my transportation advisor Jack Worley. Jack was carefully assembling over 5,000 contiguous acres just a little west of McKinney, Texas. McKinney was located north of Dallas and the county seat of Collin County, the county immediately north of Dallas County. Most signs indicated that growth and development were headed straight North and the suburbs between Dallas and McKinney only had so much land to develop. Our company could make a long-term investment like undeveloped real estate that we would have to hold for several years because of the nature of our business. Life insurance was a long-term business and the outlays in claims and surrenders were fairly predictable. Buying one small farm required a lot of talking to farmers and spitting over the fence and Jack was patient enough to be good at that.

Since Jack was the only living past president of the North Dallas Chamber of Commerce that didn't support Betty, he was an ideal advisor. Transportation was important to Jack and he spent a great deal of time working on the issues with the Texas State Highway Commission, and the Tollway Authority. The land our company was assembling wouldn't increase in value as much if Dallas and its northern suburbs end up in gridlock.

We met in Jack's office at Gulf United among all the aerial photographs of farms that Jack was negotiating to buy for Gulf United. I spotted several documents on his desk that were from the State Highway Department and several street and freeway plans from Dallas and its northern suburbs.

It was apparent that Jack was excited to discuss this subject when he stood up, then sat down. It was as if he was so excited, he couldn't sit still. "Jim, transportation should be your number one issue. The freeways and many streets are moving toward gridlock in our part of town. Not only the City of Dallas but in north Dallas County and the south Collin County suburbs."

"That certainly seems to fit my district and no one else in the campaign seems to be talking about it, at least sincerely."

Jack continued. "With transportation, you need to think on a regional basis," he said as we both looked at a huge map of the area, highlighted with possible future areas of improvement. "Of course, we need to pass the DART election for a limited version of mass transit, but we also desperately need State Highway 190 (later a tollway named for President George H.W. Bush). If I were you, I would come out immediately and call for the construction of State Highway 190 to relieve the East/West congestion."

I said. "Yeah, there is opposition but not from Dallas. I heard there's a group in one neighborhood in the suburb of Carrolton that has filed a lawsuit to oppose it. For Dallas it's a no-lose issue. It would only have a positive effect of relieving East/West congestion. God knows Dallas has done enough to help the suburbs."

Jack continued. "Yes, the Carrolton group has been able to stop it temporarily, but we can get beyond that problem eventually. The real issue will be how to pay for it. The state likes to build highways where they can get the right of way donated. While we are fighting among ourselves about whether to allow the state to build, San Antonio and Houston are offering right of way donations. Which highways get approved under those circumstances?"

"Those in San Antonio and Houston, of course."

Jack continued with another thorny issue. "Also, another area for you is that something has to be done about North Central Expressway. It was designed in the 1920's. There wasn't money for its construction during the depression of the 1930's and of course it was put on hold during World War II, and then finally built in the early 1950's. It was obsolete the day it opened. The state wants to add lanes on top of lanes or double deck it to look like Interstate 35 going through central Austin."

I interjected. "I know the neighborhoods on each side are vehemently opposed to a double deck solution. They point to the negative changes that took place close to the double decked freeway in Austin. Freeways by themselves tend to split neighborhoods and the double decked ones are worse. Those neighborhoods suffered, and property values declined. The alternative is to widen it but that won't work south of Mockingbird because of businesses located close to the freeway."

That's a perfect fit with protecting neighborhoods from excessive up zoning, which tends to bring about more traffic problems. The problem is protecting those neighborhoods from the double deck solution doesn't help with the traffic problems.

"Jack! What's the answer?"

"I don't know. If you don't double deck and you don't widen, what else is there?"

"That's a good lesson in transportation Jack, and I appreciate your advice. You've given me a lot of issues to bring up and discuss on the campaign trail."

"And problems to solve once you're elected. You gotta think positive."

"Thanks, man. You'll be my transportation advisor once elected."

"You'll need to listen to Mildred Cox, an engineer in the Transportation Department who will soon be the department head. She knows her stuff."

The next volunteer was David Johnson. I met David through our wives, both English riding fans who met at Willow Bend Polo and Hunt Club in Plano. David was a stockbroker with E.F. Hutton but more importantly was a business reporter for the public media affiliate, KERA TV and Radio. He had his own show on Friday nights where he interviewed business leaders. His show was on just before Wall Street Week, a popular predecessor of CNBC, Fox Business and the Bloomberg Business channels.

We met at Willow Bend that Friday evening. While Jetta and

David's wife Debbie took a riding lesson, David and I talked about the campaign. "I've got time and want to be involved," he said.

I breathed a sigh of relief, knowing my other possible media person was not available. "The only media consultant I know is Lisa LeMaster, who did media for Bartlett in his congressional campaign. Problem is she's running Betty's campaign, her first gig as a full campaign manager and consultant. How about being my media representative?"

"Okay. That should be a lot of fun." David's help turned out to be immeasurable with all his contacts in the media.

Enid also introduced me to Harvey Williams. Harvey was a tremendous help, a methodical guy, a manufacturer's rep who seemed to know everybody in the western part of the district. He was God sent. He was active in the Episcopal Church at Midway Road and Walnut Hill Lane, the gateway to Betty's strength.

He first volunteered to be in charge of yard sign construction. To introduce me to his workers (neighborhood and church friends), he hosted a breakfast meeting.

We met at a breakfast and lunch place called the Hungry Jockey, a small cafe tucked away in a shopping center in North Dallas. Harvey and I and five of his friends sat around the table in the back, which was semi-private. I gave his friends my pitch and they agreed to build the yard signs in Harvey's backyard. He told me to show up the morning of the construction, which I was happy to and participated in the work along with his recruited crew.

"You have to meet Alice Pesek," Harvey said, "She knows many, many people in North Dallas west of Midway Road and has been asking me to bring you over. How about tomorrow morning at her home?"

"Sure, why not."

The next morning Harvey picked me up and we went over to Alice's home. The three of us sat around her breakfast room table and drank coffee for about an hour. Alice did most of the talking, which was a non-stop tirade about how Betty Svoboda had insulted her in connection with the Crime Watch Program.

Alice pounded her fist on the table. "We can't let that woman get elected. You have to beat her. My neighborhood is counting on you. I'm not the only one she's insulted. I'll help you any way I can, anything that you need."

I slid a pledge card her way. "Alice, I'd love to have you on my steering committee. Would you please sign the card and endorse me?'

"Of course," she replied as she signed the card.

With that Harvey gave the signal. "Alice, we need to go, but you'll be invaluable. Just be yourself and talk Jim up with your friends and neighbors." With that he stood up and motioned for me to follow him out of the house.

I shook her hand with both of mine. "Alice, thank you very, very much. I'm looking forward to working with you on this campaign and after I win."

"You just better win," she said as we left.

When we reached the car Harvey said, "That woman is a live radio commercial. She will tell everybody she knows that you need to beat Betty."

"I'm lucky to have her."

I'm lucky to have Harvey.

Enid told me one day early in the campaign she was sending over Buck Wynne. "Buck is in law school at SMU but has some time to work on your campaign. He'll serve as my representative since I'm consulting for Starke Taylor's campaign for mayor. Ebby is supporting Starke and Betty has already started complaining to Starke that I'm also your campaign consultant. Even though I'm doing this as a friend, I still have to do it on the QT."

"Great! I can use all the help I can get."

Buck shows up later that day at our new campaign headquarters. "I'm here as a volunteer and as Enid's eyes and ears. Here's a personal check for a $500 contribution. Will that help?"

"Well, hell yes it will help, "I replied, "and you will too."

We were in a make-shift office one floor below Gulf United's offices in North Dallas. It was close, so I could run upstairs if there was anything urgent for me to handle. This area was to be our campaign office, so I gave Buck his own desk and telephone. Buck was a good-looking young guy who was plenty smart and wise beyond his years. Plus, it was nice to not be the youngest person around.

He began to question me as if he were interrogating a witness. "What's your platform, other than being the Non-Betty? Why should people vote for you? What do you hope to accomplish when elected?"

"It's shaping up fairly well, thanks to friends and friends of friends. My platform is basically that growth (real estate development) is fine, as long as it's planned growth and supported with good transportation facilities. By that I mean protecting the neighborhoods from over development and improving our streets and freeways."

"Sounds a little bland but we can add some spice to it later."

"There are lots of things we can do. Computerized traffic signals that can change the flow of traffic at different times of day, adding turn lanes without widening streets and of course, a rapid transit system, a combination of light rail and busses. And I'm very much in favor of State Highway 190. I seem to have that issue by myself. Plus, the tax base is growing fast enough to increase tax revenues without increasing the rates, so no tax rate increases. Finally, there's Central Expressway. Something has to be done, other than a double deck or widening. As of now, it's only something to discuss because no one has a solution."

Buck seemed a little more satisfied, "That seems to fit your district well. Let's get to work and get you elected."

Another issue was who would run the campaign office, day and night. During the day Ruth Nicholson, a wonderful person and dedicated Republican activist of Garland was Enid's choice, so we hired our first professional, at a whopping $1,000 per month. Ruth was a great addition. Since she was from Garland, there was no conflict of interest and she knew municipal elections. One of her good friends was the mayor of Garland.

Then came Marsha Hachtel. Her husband Larry was and still is, a good friend since we met at Love Field in 1967. We spent two weeks in New York City at a new employee session for the CPA firm Haskins & Sells, a predecessor firm to Deliotte Touche. Marsha was also a wonderful addition to our team. She helped Ruth run the office during the day, kept up with the important details about anyone who made a contribution or signed a support card and did many other tasks in the financial and back office functions for the campaign.

The other headquarters addition was Lisa Saeman. I met Lisa in the Bartlett campaign and knew her to be a generous person and a tireless campaigner. She ran the telephone operation at night and became an invaluable addition.

I'd previously met Dick Solo, who was serving on the board of the Dallas County Community Action Committee, after my appointment thereon was engineered by Steve Bartlett. The chairman of DCCAC appointed me to the Finance Committee because of my background in finance and accounting. Each board committee met before the board meeting on Tuesday evenings.

From that beginning Dick and I became good friends and political allies. We agreed on issues before the finance committee and the board and he volunteered to help me in my campaign with Democratic activists as well as the civic activists he knew.

"Jim, I'm going to start and chair an informal organization called "Democrats for Jim Richards."

I was thrilled. "I love it! Dick, I appreciate any help you can give me. I know Democrats tend to vote more in municipal elections than Republicans, so if you'll do that it would be wonderful. It would also be helpful if you would tell me who I need to call on personally."

Jim Oberwetter was not only the Public Affairs Officer for Hunt Oil Company he was one of the most respected political minds in North Texas, if not the whole state. Eventually Jim served as the U. S. Ambassador to Saudi Arabia during the George W. Bush administration. We had worked together in several Bartlett campaigns.

He called the next day. "Let's put your campaign together and talk about campaign platform. Come over for the Cowboy game Sunday afternoon and bring a few of the key players."

"Gee thanks, Jim. That would be great," I replied.

That Sunday David Johnson, Buck Wynne, Bill Booher and I met with Jim and under his guidance developed a platform for the campaign issues. It was pretty much obvious from all the ad-vice I'd received so far. Protect neighborhoods from overdevelopment, support the approval of Dallas Area Rapid Transit (DART), and seek more money for transportation infrastructure. Also work with the North Texas Tollway Association for the extension of the North Dallas Tollway, push for State Highway 190 and no tax rate increases. All the real estate development meant that the tax base was growing rapidly so tax revenues were growing as well and no rate increases were needed.

How do you win a low profile race for office in an urban area on a limited budget? First, our plan was to ride the wave of resentment by citizens in the northern part of Dallas of the seemingly unplanned real estate development that had outpaced the transportation infrastructure, causing major traffic problems. Was the development unplanned? We didn't know but knew that people perceived it to be unplanned and were mad about it.

Second, we also knew that Betty's temperament would likely result in a low profile race becoming a controversial high profile race that could possibly over shadow the mayoral election. We knew that when the news media reported on the race, people believed what the media said. A positive story in one of the two major papers had a multiple of the effect of a campaign ad. Our task was for me to appear to be a reasonable, level-headed candidate as compared to our opponent.

Third, we realized that because we started late, we were behind, and time was of the essence.

There was less than two months to go and every minute counted. Betty's campaign started in June and it was January before I entered the race. That was good because her campaign was slow paced. After the push to build her steering committee and raise money, there wasn't much for her to do. We hoped her current pace would continue while we timed our efforts to be completely spent when the two months were over.

To use a running analogy, you want to pace yourself to fit the distance of the race. In a marathon, you pace yourself to be able to finish the 26.22-mile distance. In a one-mile race, you want to spend as much of yourself as you can in the one mile. Betty had been running at a marathon pace which we hoped would continue while we were on the faster one-mile pace to the finish. We had to, or we would lose.

Setting up a campaign, recruiting the important volunteers and honing up on the issues were tasks that I was familiar with, having helped many candidates before. The next phase, wholesale politics or selling myself to opinion leaders and organizations was new. I'd met with opinion leaders before but that was to ask for their advice. Now I was to start selling myself or, better still, now I was to start selling folks on the cause and the main cause was to give the citizens relief from traffic congestion and ever-increasing tax rates. This next phase will require me to develop a different skill set, selling myself to build a support list. I could sell various causes and other people but wasn't that skilled in selling myself. That lack of a skill set was overcome when I realized that this campaign wasn't just about me. It was about a cause, something bigger than me.

WHOLESALE POLITICS

Seven Weeks Till Election Day

My first task was to call back all the opinion leaders and tell them I was running after all. Most of them seemed confused. First, I was considering running, then I wasn't going to run, now I was. I understood their confusion.

Even though many may have had doubts because my campaign was on, then off and finally on again, when they read about it in the newspapers, they would know it was true. It was the second week in January for an early March election. I had just restarted my candidacy and had been frantically making calls to put together a beginning list of supporters. With these calls it wasn't a matter of asking for advice as much as asking for support.

Each day when all the events I could attend were over I went back to our campaign headquarters and made calls to activists. This is the wholesale version of retail politics. I began calling a list of Republican and Democratic precinct chairs that I had obtained from those parties' respective headquarters.

A typical call went like this. "I'm Jim Richards and I'm running for the Dallas City Council, District 3. I would much appreciate your considering supporting me in this endeavor. I'm mailing you some information about me that you should receive tomorrow or the next day." I would always, always ask for their support. Most were non-committal, not especially wanting to get involved in a municipal election.

Then I would ask, "By the way, who else should I call in your precinct?" The chairs knew all the folks who helped them on election day and for other tasks. I called each night until the usual 9:00 p.m. campaign stop time.

From 9:00 p.m. till usually 11:30 p.m. I would stuff resumes and hand written personal notes in envelopes, stamp them for mailing to everyone I had spoken to that night and then proceed to the main post office where letters mailed before midnight were usually delivered in the next day's mail. I was usually in bed by midnight with a sense of accomplishment and hope. I had no trouble falling asleep.

The urgency of a two-month campaign accelerated my development of the skill sets to start selling myself and the cause. I've never been that good at selling myself, but I could be myself and sell the cause of helping neighborhoods and relieving the area of traffic problems. I came to enjoy meeting with groups and new opinion leaders. I had given my pitch so many times I was worried it was beginning to sound monotonous. It was always the first time the opinion or group leaders heard it, but to me it sounded redundant.

All the districts had been redrawn because of the 1980 census and mine, District 3, included most of the old District 3 and parts of the old District 4. My next task was to add gravitas to the support list for me, a young kid compared to the usually older age of Council members. I started with the four Council members who had represented Districts 3 and 4. Joe Haggar, Roland Tucker and Dick Smith were relatively easy. I'd known all three men for several years. Joe was part of the delegation sent to talk Grant Fitts into letting me run and I had previously visited with him.

I had toiled in Roland Tucker's campaign, with precinct work and formed a committee we called "CPA's for Roland Tucker." Dick Smith was a friend of Enid. I had already sought his advice, primarily about transportation. Dick had spearheaded an unsuccessful campaign to create a transit authority for Dallas and Fort Worth which would include rail as well as bus lines. He easily convinced me about the need for rail, which would draw the density of development into it to create ridership. The staunch conservative State Sen. John Leedom was the tossup of the four. He, like many in the Reagan wing, viewed some of us in the Bush wing with a certain degree of skepticism. By comparison, the Reagan wing was known to us as "True Believers".

I was both excited and apprehensive. I didn't think Sen. Leedom had endorsed Betty or if he would even endorse anyone. He was the last one of the big four that had represented at least one part of the district since single-member districts had been enacted.

Kay Copeland, Sen. Leedom's campaign manager and now chief of staff, became a friend of mine during the senator's re-election campaign. I telephoned his State Senate office in Austin and asked for her.

"Good morning Kay, it's Jim Richards. "How are you and what's going on in Austin?"

"Well hi yourself, Jim. We're just fine down here in the People's Republic of Austin." I had always liked Kay. She, like Sen. Leedom, was a straight shooter. You always knew where you stood with her.

"Kay, would it possible for me to talk to the Senator? I'm running for Joe Haggar's seat on the Dallas City Council and would really appreciate his support."

"Of course you are." *I never understood exactly what that phrase meant but maybe she had already heard about it.* "And it's not his or anybody else's seat. That seat belongs to the citizens of Dallas. John's on the floor for a vote but I can patch you into the phone on his desk."

"Great. Let's try that and I would like to speak to you as well."

"Call me when you finish," she said as she patched me through to the Senate floor.

"John Leedom," he answered.

I imagined John sitting at his desk in the middle of the State Senate floor. Other senators, milling around and visiting with each other waiting on a roll call vote. A few of them might be reading briefing papers or a home town newspaper. It's hard to imagine a place like that with no smart phones.

"Good Morning, Senator Leedom. Thanks for taking my call on the floor. I understand you're waiting on a roll call vote."

"We're all here but the roll call hasn't started. What can I do for you?"

"I'm running for your old seat on the Dallas City Council and your support would be much appreciated and very helpful."

"Well, I've never seen your opponent engaged in any of my grass roots campaigns, and I know you've been with me. I'll either be for you or against you, whichever will help you the most."

Now that makes a guy feel good. "I'll take for me any day. Thank you for your help."

"Sure, good luck young man."

Young man. That's what I mean about adding gravitas. I guessed my work on his campaign outweighed any skepticism he might have of me being a true believer. He knew I wasn't a staunch conservative. John Leedom was a good honest man who worked hard for the city of Dallas, Dallas County the State of Texas and conservative causes he believed in. I admired him and his endorsement meant a lot in this District. He was not only a straight shooter but one of the most intelligent people I knew.

I called John's Senate office again and asked for Kay.

She answered, "Okay, Jim. What can I do for you this time?"

"Kay, we've worked together a lot and I would really appreciate anything you can do for me. Could I have your support?"

"We have worked together and very well. I can support you but not endorse you. You can put my daughter's name on your list of supporters and all my friends will know that is me. That's what I usually do when I want to help someone but can't formerly endorse them."

"You got it. Thanks."

I never really knew why she couldn't formerly endorse me and she didn't say but I wasn't going to push it.

My next test/opportunity was the Dallas Police and Fire Fighter's Association. These first responders were held in high esteem in Northwest Dallas. Their endorsement would be invaluable. I was skeptical about getting their endorsement, with Betty being a big Poo Bah in the Neighborhood Crime Watch Organization in Northwest Dallas. I believed they would endorse her, but I was going to try anyway.

I met with them the following night. They were interviewing candidates in the association's offices in downtown Dallas and there was a committee of police and firefighters designated to interview candidates and make recommendations for endorsement. The room we were using was dimly lit and I had trouble seeing everyone. The officers on the committee were in a semi-circle facing me and several other officers were standing behind them. I was naturally nervous and this was my first chance to get an endorsement of a group like this. A seasoned firefighter asked most of the questions.

"So, Jim Richards," he began. "Tell us who you are, why you are running and what do you want to do if you're elected."

I gave my standard pitch advocating improved transportation facilities and protection of neighborhoods from high density development. It may have been a little disingenuous to conveniently forget to mention being against tax increases.

"Our big issue is the right to bargain collectively with the City. Would you be okay with being with us on that?"

This is something my research hadn't covered. I was not prepared but it seemed harmless. Why shouldn't they be able to bargain like any other interest group? "Yeah sure, I would be okay with your right to bargain collectively."

Everyone in the room looked surprised. Attendees started exchanging glances around the room and whispering to the people sitting next to them. I knew I had said something that was important to them and hoped it wouldn't end up as a negative in the campaign. The moderator quickly changed the subject. "Okay, do you know anyone in our Association? Do you know any police officers? Do you know any firefighters?"

I paused briefly, then remembered. "Yes, my best friend from the second grade through high school is a Dallas firefighter. His name is Milton Petty. I haven't seen him since he broke the heart of one of my wife's good friends."

"Anyone here know Milton Petty?" asked the moderator. A firefighter in the back of the crowd spoke up. "I do and it sounds just like that rascal Milton. You wife's friend isn't the only broken heart around here."

"Okay Jim Richards, you'll hear from us after we've made a decision."

I left the room, went home and called Enid.

"You agreed to what? To their right to bargain collectively? They've wanted that right for years. They want to form a union. That's what it means. Call the leader back first thing tomorrow and recant. The Citizens Council, the Dallas Chamber of Commerce, the North Dallas Chamber of Commerce and most the Republicans in your District will have a hissy fit."

The next day with my stomach knotted up I called the leader back. "I'm sorry but I have to change my answer about collective bargaining. I would not be okay with it." I felt pretty good as I left the meeting the night before but now, I had really blown it this time.

"That's okay," he replied. "We knew you'd probably have to come off that stand and decided to endorse you anyway. We have to get the state law changed to have that right and we're working that angle. The City Council can't just vote it in for us. Also, your opponent is hard to get along with. In the past she's insulted several members of the police force in connection with her role in the Neighborhood Crime Watch Organization. She thinks she knows more than the average police officer."

I was relieved. "Thank you for your support, and I'll give every consideration to the issues that are important to you." I dodged a bullet with these guys. I thought for sure that Betty's work in crime watch would be enough to gain their endorsement but just the opposite happened.

In addition to the first opinion leaders list, Enid had another list of names for me to approach early in the campaign, partially to build a support list. "You need to meet with insurance executive Tom Dunning, as early as you can get in. He's active in several civic organizations and his endorsement would be super. He's also rumored to be considering a run himself, so go see him as soon as you get a chance."

I placed a call immediately. "Tom, it's Jim Richards. I'd like to come see you about the race for District 3 on the City Council. Would you be able to make time for me to come by?"

"That council race is an interesting situation. How about tomorrow afternoon about 3:00? Do you know where my office is?"

"Sure, and I'll be there at 3:00."

I arrived a few minutes early and was ushered in by his administrative assistant. One thing I noticed right away was a partner's desk, where Tom and his business partner sat side by side. I'd seen several partners' desks before, but the ones I had seen had the partners' facing each other like my favorite, a World War II British field officer's desk.

"Come in and have a seat," Tom said. "Why do you want to talk about the race?" Tom was known as a genuinely good guy. His office was decorated with awards for civic activity.

I responded. "You live in the district. Are you considering running?"

"Not at this time. I'm pretty tied up here with my work. Besides, who wants to get in front of a Betty Svoboda steamroller driven by Ebby Halliday?"

I laughed out loud. *What a great political cartoon it would make. A steam roller that looked like Betty snarling at every one with Ebby Holliday*

Tom continued, "Ebby has already been here asking that I
support Betty. It's hard to turn her down but at least I was able to
resist temporarily. Tell me who you are and why do you ask?"

"I'm interested in running myself. I'm a businessman and have
been politically active in several campaigns, including the last bond
election. I've done a lot of civic work, including serving on the board
of two half way houses in Dallas. I've served as an appointed member
of the Dallas County Community Active Agency, which administers
all the War on Poverty grants and on the Civil Service Board for the
City of Dallas. If you're not going to run I would appreciate your
support for me. How about it?"

Tom laughed. "You and Betty Svoboda?" He sure emphasized the
"you" as if I were a lamb going to slaughter. "Interesting." Tom
laughed even louder, as if the thought of someone, especially a young
guy like me, taking on a steam roller was quite funny. "I'll think about
it. Thanks for coming by and good luck."

With that abrupt dismissal I stood up, turning toward the door.
"Well thank you for visiting with me and I hope to have your
support." I had the perception he was laughing me out of his office,
so I left.

Bob Folsom had been president of the Dallas School Board of
Trustees and then was mayor of Dallas from 1976 to 1981. He
seemed to be a phenomenal success at everything he touched. West
Point, Southern Methodist University education and sports, elected
office and business. He was a major real estate developer.

His most visible project was the development of the Bent Tree
neighborhood in Far North Dallas, formerly the town of Renner. His
name on my support list would go well, right next to the four
previous holders of this office. I called for an appointment and was
granted one for two o'clock the next afternoon.

I rode the elevator up to his office, located near the Dallas North Tollway in Bent Tree area. It was in a three-office building complex that he developed. His outer office was huge, with beautiful Persian rugs on hardwood floors. I walked up to the receptionist and introduced myself. "Good afternoon Ms. I'm Jim Richards to see Mr. Folsom."

She smiled back with a "Why yes. I'll let him know you're here."

In a few minutes she emerged from his office and said, "You can go in now. Would you like anything to drink? Coffee, soft drink, perhaps?"

"No thank you, Ma'am, I'm just fine."

Bob looked up and set aside a stack of papers he was reading. "Come in and have a seat."

He was sitting behind a huge desk and in front of a large floor to ceiling window overlooking the tollway and the Bent Tree neighborhood.

"Mayor Folsom, I'm running for the Dallas City Council District 3 and would love to have your support. I'm a business man and worried about traffic gridlock. I believe our transportation issues are regional issues, not local, and should be addressed on a regional basis. I'm in favor of State Highway 190 to the north to relieve East/West congestion in North Dallas and of course the DART for rapid transit. Whether elected or not, I will work hard to get the DART election passed."

Leaning forward toward me, he replied, "Go on."

"There are things we can do on a local basis. We need money in the next bond election to build streets. Period. Computerized traffic signal systems, extra turn lanes, and extension of the Dallas North Tollway to Plano will also help."

"You seem to be the kind of Council candidate willing to listen to other people. Where else would you have gotten those ideas?"

"Yes, straight from Jack Worley and Sid Stahl."

"Well, you have wise people advising you and seem to be focused on solutions, not just problems. What about Central Expressway?"

"As you probably know, the state wants to double deck. Surrounding neighborhoods vehemently oppose that and we can't widen south of Mockingbird because of the proximity of business firms to the right of way. It's a riddle inside of a puzzle inside of an enigma and I don't have a solution. I will promise you to make it a priority and find a solution while I'm in office. There's got to be a transportation engineering firm that can come up with something outside of the box."

"That's an honest response. I will support you. Leave a pledge/ donation card with my secretary. Thank you for coming by, young man."

"Thank you for seeing me and for your support."

With that, I knew to leave his office. He probably had already made up his mind and just wanted to meet me before finalizing the decision. Really enjoyed the view, though. *Maybe someday I would have an office like that.*

The first Democratic group Dick put me in front of was the local chapter of the National Organization of Women (NOW). I was completely unprepared for their questions, which were focused on abortion. Regretfully, my answers were uninformed.

The moderator quickly dismissed me with a "Well, thanks for coming by. At least you showed up when your opponent didn't."

I had thought they would be more interested in local issues than in social politics. That was a humiliating experience and it taught me a lesson to be better prepared. Some folks in political situations put their feet in their mouth time after time and never learn from the experience. I came away determined not to go through that experience again.

On another level, I should have understood their perspective.

Dick had arranged for me to speak to them and I had taken it too lightly. They have an agenda and that agenda is important to them. No, it wasn't traffic, potholes, the tax rate, zoning or any of the things I was questioned about every day, but it was their particular concerns. I should have had a more nuanced conversation with them, recognizing their agenda.

CREATING A SENSE OF URGENCY

Each day our modest space looked more like a real campaign headquarters, with desks, chairs, telephones and even a few volunteers. Fred Stern, one of my transplant to Texas friends, came to our campaign headquarters one day early in the process to get involved. Fred started developing a stump speech for me, using the pitch I'd given to each opinion leader and then building on that by including phrases that would appeal to a broader audience, especially senior citizens who made up most of the voters in the district. Fred was a talented speech writer. He took the speech that Buck Wynne thought was too bland and spiced it up.

What to do about Central Expressway was an issue on many folk's mind. I had discussed the issue in depth with Jack Worley during our conversation about transportation and there wasn't an apparent solution. It never failed that if I went to a meeting anywhere close to Central Expressway the question came up, I tried to answer by explaining the alternatives and stating that a solution hasn't been found yet but there's got to be one out there and I'm determined to find it.

Fred, along with Buck, was an early version of a campaign manager. "You need a new brochure and we have to develop one. It needs to have pictures. Do you know a photographer?"

"My wife's sister, Patty, is an amateur photographer but that's as close as I can come."

"She'll be fine. See if she can be available tomorrow so we can photograph you at City Hall, meeting with Joe Haggar and Roland Tucker. The Council meets tomorrow. It will make you look like you belong there. Then let's go by a fire station and show your support for our first responders."

Sure enough, the next day we found the two outgoing Council members at City Hall. Patty took photos of me shaking their hands in front of the horseshoe like structure that the City Council sat behind during formal meetings. Each place along the horseshoe contained a microphone controlled by the presiding officer of the meetings, which was usually the mayor. Then we shot one with me standing behind the horseshoe as if I belonged there and then one coming out of the Council offices. Being there in the area where the debates took place was exciting and increased my determination to win, which was my only real competitive advantage. I could feel myself being there, behind the horseshoe, being part of the debates. I wanted to go out and campaign 24-7 until the polls were closed and all the votes were cast. Winning would allow me to become the advocate for improved transportation infrastructure that was desperately needed. Winning would allow me to work with my colleagues to stop tax rate increases that were funding an ever larger bureaucracy at City Hall. Winning would allow me to help protect neighborhoods from excessive development.

After that, we found a fire station with its bay doors open for a photo by the fire trucks. There was also a police cruiser nearby and a couple of officers inside. After I told them that their association endorsed me. They stood by me and the cruiser for a photo shoot. A fire station didn't have quite the same effect as City Hall but it didn't matter. I was fired up enough already.

David Johnson's first task as my media consultant was to organize a press conference. He was waiting at headquarters and discussing the campaign with Buck and Ruth when Fred and I returned from City Hall.

David was ready to make something happen. "We need to have a press conference to announce your candidacy. I will make some calls to get reporters there and reserve a space at Union Station for tomorrow morning."

"Great idea," I said. Union Station was the old downtown train station that had been restored for events such as this. "The only announcement I've made was on the day I filed. I attended the Republican Men's Club luncheon that day. After Dan Garrigan, the club president, introduced all the office holders and other candidates, he asked if there were any more in attendance. I stood and answered that I had just filed a few minutes ago and was running." We had set it up that way in advance to get a little more exposure.

David continued. "This announcement will reach a lot more people. I'm going to need a list of your supporters and a political resume. Several copies of both will be necessary. I'll pick you up in the morning for a 10:00 a.m. press conference."

"I'll be ready." I had a running list of supporters already and had recently updated my resume, which showed my work experience and campaigns that I had been involved in, emphasizing the two city boards I had served on and the municipal campaigns I had volunteered for.

David picked me up at headquarters and prepped me on the way down. "Be confident and hope your conference will generate some media questions. When we arrive, I'll go up and check out the room and you wait downstairs until exactly 10:00. Then come up to the room for the conference."

The room where I waited was the huge downstairs lobby for the building, which at one time was the lobby of the Dallas railroad station, which was named Dallas Union Station. There were few people in the lobby and I stood for a moment imagining what it would have been like there before air transportation. The lobby must have been buzzing with noise. People buying tickets, meeting friends and relatives who were arriving, or struggling with large suitcases, running to catch a train. Children with runny noses fidgeting or asleep next to their parents sitting on old wooden benches. Cigarette butts and crumbled up papers scattered thoughtlessly on the old brick floor.

I sort of lost track of time and missed the 10:00 a.m. start. When I realized I was a few minutes late I bounded up the stairs and made my way into the room. Some reporters looked up from reading my bio/resume and the list of supporters. The room was a good size, small enough that it seemed full. There were no chairs in the room so everyone stood. A few flags guarded one corner of the room. I recognized the City of Dallas flag but couldn't see the other two. Must have been Old Glory, the U.S. flag and the Lone Star, the flag of the State of Texas.

David chose a day when nothing was scheduled at City Hall so there would be no conflicts. There was a good turnout. In addition to the scheduling, David must have called in some chits. ABC and NBC affiliates were there with television cameras. City Hall beat writers from both newspapers were there.

Seeing the press there made me feel relevant. Other than the television camera operators, who were grizzled veterans, they all looked young like me, although more casually dressed. It was not only exciting, I actually felt like a real candidate. There were TV and radio reporters there to see me and hear what I had to say and answer their questions. David had been ready to start for a few minutes.

"Okay, let's get started everyone. Here is Jim Richards, candidate for District 3 on the Dallas City Council. Jim, you have the floor."

No applause, although none expected. I was enthusiastic. "Hello, I'm Jim Richards, the candidate. Thank you for coming." With that I briefly went over my bio and then gave my newly developed stump speech, emphasizing protecting neighborhoods, solving traffic problems and efficient city operations so as to save tax dollars. "I don't have a problem with growth and development, as long as it's planned growth and careful development to protect our existing neighborhoods. We have a traffic problem in the City but it's a regional problem. We're a central city sur- rounded by suburbs. Much of our traffic comes in each morning and leaves in the afternoon so transportation is a regional problem and needs a regional solution. Dallas Area Rapid Transit or DART is part of that solution and I'm here to work with officials in our neighboring cities to find the others."

In graduate school at UT Dallas I specialized in Unban/Regional Political Economy and wanted to be recognized as a person with a larger perspective.

The speech took about five minutes. Then David asked for questions.

The first question was from a newspaper beat reporter who knew of most of the people on my list. "I've never seen such an ideologically diverse support list. Are you sure folks on the conservative Republican side know they are on the same list as folks on the liberal Democrat side and vice a versa?"

I felt myself stiffen, I had always thought of these folks as people I had made friends with while serving in some capacity and believed there was virtue in having an ideologically diverse group.

David quickly stepped in to help. "Thank you for the compliment. I'm sure Jim is proud of his appeal across the political spectrum."

I responded. "These are folks I have worked with on campaigns, collaborated on civic issues, served on boards and commissions with and fellow church members. They know me, not for a political ideology but as a worker for good causes."

Another reporter spoke, "I'm referring to Betty's formal announcement. She says she has the support from W.C. (Dub) Miller, Doug Fain, Bill Nicol, Juanita Craft and L.A. Murr; five former Council members. How are you going to counter that?"

My retort was quick. "My list of supporters includes Councilman Joe Haggar, who currently represents District 3 and since the District includes part of the old District 4, my support list also includes Councilman Roland Tucker, the current Council member from District 4. In addition, my supporters include the predecessors of those two gentlemen, Texas State Sen. John Leedom from District 3 and Dick Smith from District 4. That means that every Dallas City Council member who has served those two districts since the inception of single-member districts in 1975 serves on my steering committee, as well as an at-large Council member, Sid Stahl and a former mayor, Bob Folsom. I believe the folks in her announcement included former members who either represented other districts or were at-large."

Then came the perennial question. "Why are you running?"

"I'm tired of the potholes, crowded streets and traffic jams just like everybody else, including you and I want to try to help fix it." My answer got a lot of laughs.

"Mr. Richards, what are you going to do about East/West traffic in North Dallas?"

"The problem is regional. The regional area is no longer folks living in the north and south and driving to the central business district to work. On a regional basis, most live East and work in the West. That means the morning commute is westbound and the evening commute is eastbound. The answer to that problem is regional. The answer is to take a lot of the East/West traffic out of the picture. It's time for the suburbs that are creating the traffic, to absorb some of that traffic. I'm supporting the proposed East/West freeway to be located north of Dallas called State Highway 190. The State Department of Highways and Public Transportation has proposed building the highway but a neighborhood near the projected site in Carrolton has filed a lawsuit delaying but hopefully not stopping the project. That proposed freeway will relieve some of the East/West traffic congestion. Additional city streets are needed in Far North Dallas and that will help as well. *Thank you Jack Worley, my transportation mentor, for that piece of advice.*

The next question was actually a compliment, of sorts. "You have been quite politically active in the past, unlike many folks who run for this office. Are you just interested in City Hall or is there something else on the horizon down the road?"

I had been alerted to have an answer or an acceptable non answer for that one. "Tm just announcing a race for the first time. I'm a business man who has been involved in a lot of civic activities as well, and I believe I can help solve some of the transportation and other problems of our city. That's my focus now and in the foreseeable future."

David was standing among the media members to give the impression that he was one of them but also situated where I could see him. He nodded, as if for me to go on.

I did. "I'm attracted to municipal government. I believe the closer government is to the people, the better to serve the people. Representatives in Washington don't see their constituents as part of their everyday activities. They're too distant from their districts to have a feel for what people are thinking. Municipal governments have more direct effect of citizens than any other level of government. They provide streets and enforce the rules of driving. They keep the peace and put out the fires. They provide water and sewer services. They educate our children. They regulate land use so that someone doesn't build a convenience store in the middle of a single-family neighborhood. They provide physical and mental health care for the indigent. Now some of that effect is school district and county, but it's still local government. As a member of the City Council, I will work with Dallas Independent School Board Trustees and the Dallas County judge and commissioners for the betterment of this area."

I had spoken with the emotion that I was feeling at the time. I believed local government was important and wished others realized it as well. The citizens of Dallas may not realize it because these things have run quite well in North Texas in the past and people usually notice in cities where city services as a whole are not being taken care of.

The reporter seemed satisfied with that answer.

Next question was sort of accusatory. "Ms. Svoboda says she's heard for the past six months of the campaign about efforts to recruit a businessman to run against her. Who recruited you to run and who else did they talk to?"

"I'm not sure who 'they' are. I know there is some dissatisfaction with Ms. Svoboda, that some think she is too conservative and too outspoken. No one recruited me to run against her. I'm in the race because I want to be. I'm in the race because I'm interested in City affairs. I'm in the race to do something about our crowded streets and highways."

The reporter nodded and scribbled. Then spoke. "I bring this up because Ms. Svoboda declared, 'I'm running my own race, and if they recruited Richards, that's their problem because I'm going to whip him'." A few of the reporters chuckled. "So, Mr. Richards, do you have a response?"

By that time everyone in the room was actively paying attention as the intensity level increased, not just the group of reporters who were jotting things down but several folks who heard the conversation from other parts of the building and had gathered. This kind of attention was an example of how the race eventually became the darling of the media's attention.

I answered back, "Again, she uses the word 'they' without naming anyone, as if she's created a group in her mind, like a straw man to complain about. Look, I'm a sports fan. So many times folks will say one team looks so much better on paper than their next opponent and that they are sure winners. There are no sure winners; that's why we play the game, to see who can perform in the real world. Ms. Svoboda may look better on paper now because she has a six-month head start, has Ebby Halliday on her side and has probably raised more money than I have. But like I said, we have to play the game and see who can perform. I was considering the race last summer, and she called me then to discourage me from running. She told me, 'you don't stand a chance so don't waste your time'. That call and her comments tell me she is worried about the race."

I had given them enough to make it a lively race. Since there were no more questions, David closed things out. "Looks like we're done here. Thanks to everybody for coming."

"That went well. Betty didn't even have a formal press conference to announce. She may have sent a statement to the media outlets by fax." David told me on the way out.

The challenge of the back and forth with reporters at the press conference was fun and exciting. In a campaign with many ups and downs, that was certainly an up. I liked my answers and was glad for the questions that gave me an opportunity to express things that had been building up, mostly related to Betty's arrogance. Based on this morning's activities, I believed that this low-profile race was going to be more interesting to the news media than most of the others and it was about to become high profile. My self-confidence was boosted, and I couldn't wait to get back to campaigning.

Many issues are introduced to candidates when the two daily newspapers hit the sidewalks each morning. Today was no exception. The phone rang at 7:00 a.m. I had been up for an hour. It was Enid.

"Look in the metro section of the *Dallas Morning News* this morning. There's an article about the police department and the Dallas gay community. Chief Billy Prince has taken a stand against gays on the police force. He probably reacted because his officers, through the police association, were complaining."

I opened my paper to the metro section and spotted the article immediately. "I see it. So?"

"The reporters caught Betty off guard. They asked her what she thought of the idea of having gays on the police force without telling her that the chief was against it."

"I see her quote now. She doesn't have a problem with it."

"Rumor has it that upon hearing that the chief was against it, she tried to change her mind. That's two constituencies she angered the gay community for so quickly going back on her word and the Dallas Police Association who were opposed to the idea. Now that they have her quote, they're probably about to reach out to you. What are you going to say?"

"I have nothing against the idea of gays serving on the force; they should be allowed. But that's not the real issue. The real issue is supporting the chief. This district is very supportive of the police department and especially the police chief, and this chief is well liked by the force itself."

"Okay, go on. What is your position?"

"Dallas has a long tradition of following the rules of a council-manager form of municipal government. The City Charter draws a line that separates the authority and responsibilities of the mayor and Council on one side and the city manager on the other. The police chief reports to the city manager. Furthermore, he or she should be able to run the police department without having to deal with a mayor and ten City Council members second guessing him."

"Go on."

"If the mayor and council don't like positions taken by the chief, the proper avenue for that complaint is to the city manager, who selects the police chief. Our personal positions of every issue shouldn't be interjected with the mix." I didn't mention that the Council was elected to make political decisions, and this was clearly a political decision.

"Good. You're learning already. Their next question will be to ask you again what your position is."

"And my answer is that I believe the police chief should be making these decisions and any personal preferences I may have should be directed to the city manager."

"Since Betty took the position that she is in favor I have some latitude to let folks guess my position. I will say that I will express any reservations I have on that or any other issue with the city manager."

"Good. You are the young candidate and with that response you don't alienate the gay community, many of which live in your district and yet the Citizens Council receives a message that you are supportive of the council-manager form of government and won't try to cross over that boundary separating the elected officials from the bureaucracy, which many do with results that are controversial, at best."

When we hung up the phone rang immediately. George Rodrigue, the City Hall reporter for the *Dallas Morning News* called me. He confronted me with the question and told me what Betty's response was. "What is your position about having gays on the police force? Your opponent is fine with it."

I gave him a duplicate of my answer to Enid.

That ended the issue as far as the campaign was concerned. The police thought that Betty was in favor of having gays on the police force. Gay voters may have thought that she didn't since she tried to change her mind. Neither was sure where I was except for supporting the police chief and the council-manager form of government. However, since I supported the chief and the chief was against gays, the newspaper stories had me as being opposed as well.

The council-manager form of municipal government was near and dear to the City's business establishment. The Council members and the mayor were only paid a token fifty dollars a meeting and as far as the establishment was concerned that reduced the number of candidates that considered it a full-time job with full time pay. It tended to attract more "civic minded" folks because Council members had less direct power, unlike a ward system for a city like Chicago where alderman have the power to decide who gets particular jobs and other appointments. Each candidate was to be interviewed by the executive director of the Citizens Council and asked about these issues.

I was well versed as to how this form of government worked simply from following the news as described in the two local newspapers and from many discussions among activists and city board and commission members. My interview was scheduled for the next day, so I benefited from this sort of rehearsal.

When my day for the Citizens Council interview came I reported to the place where the interview was scheduled. It was an austere building downtown and the offices inside were almost bare, at least where the interviews took place. When my time came, Alex Bickley, the executive director, or the top paid employee asked the questions. He was the only person in attendance meaning the Citizens Council would only know what Alex wanted them to know. Alex was a former city attorney and knew the issues that his organization cared about. He was dressed in a black suit, white shirt, black shoes and a very narrow black tie, 1950's vintage. No preppy look for him. If he had a cap he could have passed for a limo driver. Alex sneered at me as he welcomed me to the interview. He began with "Jim Richards, do you support the current council-manager form of government?"

So, this was the infamous Alex Bickley. I heard that he was suspicious of any candidate under 50 years old. He wrinkled his brow, lowered his head and stared at me, as if waiting for me to say something stupid.

"Yes, of course I do. That's one of the reasons I'm running. I support the system and would like to help all I can to retain it and keep it strong."

He's looking up from his script at me with surprise written all over his face. What was he expecting me to say, no, I don't believe in it? We need a ward system like Chicago.

Alex shook his head and turned away so I couldn't see the expression on his face. He must have been expecting a different answer, which he probably got from some of the younger candidates. Alex finally got over his surprise and asked his second question. "And do you believe City Council members and the mayor should be paid more than $50 per week?

"No, of course not. That would invite all the riff raff who want to run and hold office just for the money and we don't need that. I have a job and will serve the citizens and make my own living outside of City Hall." Although I was likely to lose my job when our company sold, that was next year's problem or two years away. I did have a job at the present time.

"And do you support the current 8-3 districting scheme with eight single-member districts, two at-large Council members and the mayor with the three representing the whole city?

"Of course. Somebody needs a whole city perspective. Actually, we potential single-member district representatives are elected from particular districts but are supposed to represent the whole City just like the mayor and the at-large members."

With that answer the interview was over, and I got the usual send off. "Well that wraps it up. Good luck to you, young man."

Many folks say that perception is reality in politics. I will go a step farther and say the perception is reality in many more things. Alex's perception of 30 something candidates running in single-member districts (like me) would not only be more inclined to represent neighborhoods than real estate developers but also be in favor of abandoning the council-manager form of city government.

A fundamental problem with that notion is that the alternative to council-manager is having a strong mayor; who actually runs the bureaucracy, appoints department heads as well as having political patronage. In the strong mayor form of municipal government, the Council members have even less power over polity than in the council-manager form.

I smiled as I left his office and gave everyone I ran into on the way out a pleasant "Hello, how are you."

I don't know what Alex will tell his board and membership about the District 3 race but if he interviews Betty, I believe the worse he will be is neutral.

I began to realize that I had an ability to do what Jim Oberwetter calls "think politically," meaning the ability to understand what folks' reaction will be to what is written, said or done. I used to think that everyone can, but he said that's not the case. Anyway, it could have come from my mother, whose parents both died when she was young. She had to learn to live with relatives and get along without being an immediate family member. It could have come from my years in the corporate world and navigating among folks who I had to get along with, even if we disagreed. No matter where it came from, it's going to come in handy now.

I had started walking the district door to door. I believed my walking was going to be the deciding factor if I met enough people. I liked meeting people and listening to their complaints and ideas about what needed to be done. I looked forward to being in a position to be able to work with people and resolve differences or negotiate an agreement of some kind. I can meet enough people if I have enough time to campaign. Wish I could have started sooner but the time remaining is what it is and I had to take advantage of very minute.

RETAIL POLITICS

Six Weeks Till Election Day

Trying to map out a strategy for the campaign, Buck and I met at headquarters. Ruth was on board as the campaign headquarters manager and Marsha Hachtel was on top of the fund raising. There were desks in the large room we called the bullpen and several desks had telephones. There were stacks of computer printouts of frequent municipal voters for phone calls and precinct walks. A few volunteers came by from time to time to see if there were any envelopes to stuff or phone calls to make.

Buck set the stage for our discussion. "Okay, it's mid-January and the election is the first Saturday in March. That's not a lot of time to campaign and you're going to have to go from a 7:00 a.m. breakfast meeting till 9:00 p.m. at night, every day, including election day. You're starting behind, big time. How are you going to win, having started this late? What's your strategy, what's your competitive advantage?"

I gave him a quizzical look "What do you mean?"

"What can or will you do that she cannot do, or will not do, for the six weeks remaining in the campaign? What will make up for her six months head start? What will make up for Ebby's support? Think about that."

"Yes, Ebby is her competitive advantage." Buck stood up and turned toward me, as if to make sure I took this seriously. "She lends prestige to Betty's campaign, recruits supporters and raises money. Betty is smart and knows a lot about the City and how city government works."

I kept assuring him. "Don't think that point hasn't been hammered into me. There's an advantage to being behind."

"Are you sure about that?"

"Yes. She doesn't think she has to do anything. First, she probably believes that she will make a much better Council member and the people will recognize that and vote for her. Second, she is way ahead. Oh, she will send out a couple of mailers and attend all the North Dallas Chamber of Commerce meetings and maybe a few other campaign functions. But that's it," I said, and a smile crept across my face.

Buck nodded. "Go on. What else?"

"She doesn't have Enid Gray, Buck Wynne, David Johnson, Bill Booher, Fred Stern, Ruth Nicholson, Lisa Saeman, Dick Solo or Marsha Hachtel."

"Okay, what are you going to do?" Buck asked.

"There is something that I can do that she probably won't do or won't think she needs to do. I'm going to walk the district, knock on doors and meet people, concentrating on the frequent municipal voter households that Enid has targeted, so as not to waste any time, which I have little of."

"Now we're talking."

"In a low-profile race like this, if a voter meets one candidate in person and not the other, they are most likely to vote for the one that they have met. It can be more important than gender, party affiliation, ideology, or charisma."

"That might work, if you're willing to do it. Do you think you can stick with it?" Buck asked, with a shrug.

"I have no choice. Little money and no cadre of volunteers or North Dallas Chamber heavies. Plus, I really want to win. She's convinced that she's going to win. I'm determined to win."

"I've known a lot of candidates who start out saying they're going to walk their district, then quit after about a week and go on to lose the election. I have a law school class this afternoon. Think about whether you are willing to do it while I'm gone. Because if you're not willing to walk, then we need a different strategy."

"I hear you loud and clear," I said as Buck left for his class. I wondered if he ever had time to study. I looked back over my life and reflected on the roots of my work ethic.

I spent many a summer working for my father, as a helper, beginning at about nine or ten years old. He was a student at Texas A&M for a year. He played semiprofessional baseball for a while and ended up in business as a wholesaler of petroleum products such as gasoline, motor oil, grease and paint. His business structure included many overhead tanks, a warehouse, an office and a delivery truck. I became his right hand man for 10 cents an hour or a dollar a day for a ten hour day. When we weren't on the road Dad stayed in his office doing paperwork in the mornings and playing dominoes with his customers and friends during the afternoon. I would fill the tanks on the back of the truck with gasoline, diesel fuel or kerosene. In between tasks, I was free to play on the huge overhead storage tanks surrounding his warehouse. The tanks were connected with two inch iron pipes and I loved to walk from one overhead tank to the other on those two inch pipes, which were about 50 feet above ground. The possibility of falling that far made each walk exciting. This is one of my earliest memories of what I now know was an adrenaline rush.

My father first let me steer the truck, and then when my legs were long enough I was allowed to drive his truck out in the country. When I reached the ripe old age of eleven my mother took me out in the country to teach me how to drive.

"Mom, I know how to drive already. I've been driving Daddy's truck for two years."

"You what? You drove his truck?" She glared but didn't say anything else. *I imagined she was saying something stronger to herself.*

My parents didn't argue in front of my sister and me but there must have been some scolding. The next morning at breakfast my father voiced his usual retort to my mom's displeasure. "I'm moving to the garage. It's time to move and I'm moving out there." Of course, he never did and I knew he never would.

After several summers of making a dollar a day and mowing lawns for 25 cents an hour, by 1957, at age 12, I knew it was time to get my own wheels. I had saved up $85 to buy a Jeep. Willis didn't make them anymore but there were many left over from World War II. Dad and I couldn't find a Jeep but he found a car for sale that I could afford; a 1931 Ford Model A, a five window coupe. Dad and I went to pick it up. We paid the old farmer who was happy to get rid of it. We pushed it off with the truck until the engine started then I drove it back to town by myself.

I couldn't afford much gasoline and really couldn't afford to buy a new battery but the car was light enough for a couple of kids to push off, then jump in, put it in gear and the momentum turned the engine over enough to start it. I could even use the hand crank if pushing off wasn't an option. The hand crank could be dangerous. You have to start the crank at the six o'clock position, pull up and make sure you pull it out at 12:00 for a half rotation. If the engine starts with the crank in place it will likely take off your hand or come flying out and hit your head.

My paternal grandfather had worked at Darsey's General Merchandise as his full-time job and my father worked there as well while growing up. When I was thirteen a Saturday job opened up at Darsey's store. I was one of two guys who sacked groceries and helped customers carry bags of groceries to their cars or pickup trucks.

My pay in that first real job was a tremendous boost from 10 cents an hour to 40 cents an hour or four dollars for a ten-hour day. At the end of each Saturday, Charlie Darsey, who ran the store would pay us in cash, $3.88 net after deducting 12 cents for social security. The job at Darsey's provided me with enough income to make ten dollars a month payments on a 1949 Chevrolet hatchback sedan.

After a couple of years stocking shelves at Darsey's, another summer job opened up at Jinx Well's gas station and this one had three advantages. It paid 50 cents an hour, nice raise for a fifteen-year-old. I could work six and a half days a week instead of six and it involved cars. I spent the summer at the station and made enough money for a paint job, chrome lake pipes and chrome hub caps. My

1949 Chevy was now a thing of beauty and envied by all the other car guys in town. My work at the gas station extended to everyday after school (or after football practice), Saturday and Sunday afternoons. I did this for the next four years.

My favorite job as a kid came the next summer. Troy Jones was an oil field contractor who built drilling locations, the cleared out areas where a drilling rig could be set up, and the roads to reach them. He also furnished roustabouts for repair work and to lay pipe from wells to tank batteries and from tank batteries to salt water disposal wells. The pay was minimum wage, which was $1.25 per hour, with time and a half for overtime. I was even reluctant to return to college that Fall.

My first taste of entrepreneurship came one summer when Jinx Wells passed away. I was 19 at the time. My father, who owned the land and building for the gas station, borrowed $ 1,000 from the Grapeland State Bank, bought the inventory from Jinx's widow and told me if I paid it off the note the station was mine. I loved every minute of every day that summer, knowing I was building the business back. Our sales tripled, I paid back the loan and again didn't want to go back to college. Dad sold the station at the end of the summer for a nice profit which helped with the cost of college.

I worked at the Lufkin Foundry in the welding shop as a sheer operator helper for a while in college. It was the 4:00 p.m.to 12:30 a.m. shift and believe me, I was sleep deprived. In my first job after college, working a 70 or 80-hour week at Deliotte Haskins & Sells, CPAs was routine. I was conditioned to work long hours.

I wasn't intellectually advanced and graduated from a small school, Stephen F. Austin State College. I believed I had to work harder than anyone else to get ahead. At the firm, my clients were probably some of the most exciting in the Dallas office and I appreciated that I was chosen to handle them. The long hours continued after I left the accounting firm and moved to Gulf United, and I thrived on working as many hours as were necessary whenever we needed to issue securities in a stock or bond offering or circulate a proxy statement for a merger. I spent many a night at a printer's office in New York City with accountants, lawyers and investment bankers as we finalized the legal documents for a stock or bond offering.

Hard work was second nature to me. Walking the district was my plan and I looked forward to doing it.

Buck finally returned, and my recollections were over. I was prepared and determined.

"Buck, we don't need another strategy. Besides, I'm not sure there is one. I'm going to walk the district every day, seven days a week, including election day."

"Okay, buddy. Do that and you have a chance to win. A chance, not a sure thing. It's going to take determination, you know."

"I'm told that's my longest and strongest suit. It sure ain't looks, intelligence, wealth or charisma."

There were usually events to attend or potential contributors to call on in the mornings, so each day's walk would start early afternoon. I would grab a list of frequent voter households sorted by street. These folks were the most likely to vote in the next election. My campaign not only mailed a brochure to them but, knowing that folks are more likely to vote for the person they've met, especially if that candidate makes an effort to visit them. This was my only competitive advantage, I wanted to meet as many folks in person as I could.

Walking relaxed me. I had been a runner for several years but didn't have time to run during the campaign. Walking precincts was a good substitute for running and filled that craving I had for exercise. I would park my car and go up one side of the street knocking on doors of selected households and then worked the other side of the street.

I started in the western part of the district, on Betty's side, and then worked my way East, knowing that I probably had a better chance with those in the east after taking out an ad in the local Jewish newspaper listing all my Jewish endorsements, led by at-large City Councilman Sid Stahl.

The voter list would of course have names. My pitch sounded like this.

"Hello, I'm Jim Richards, a candidate for the Dallas City Council, District 3. I'm 37 years old and a business man and would like to represent this neighborhood at City Hall. Do you have any complaints about the City government? Do you have any questions for me? Would you like some information? Here is a brochure with information about me."

For those that were home everyone was at least half way receptive. Typical complaints were traffic congestion, potholes in the streets, increasing tax rates and slow police response times. Not everyone was at home and some who were didn't answer the door. For those stops I would write a personal note on the brochure and then hang it on the door knob. My friends in the neighborhoods told me that once I had hit a few precincts, folks started talking about the guy who was walking door to door.

As they ran into their friends and acquaintances they would say "Has the guy running for the City Council been by your house yet? He stopped at ours and talked to my husband and me. Nice young man. Look for him. He should be in your neighborhood soon. I heard he started in the western part and is moving East."

Mid-January weather in North Texas isn't always pleasant but I was so into the campaign I hardly noticed the weather. Lucky for me it wasn't a wet winter and there were not a lot of hazardous, uneven, poorly lit sidewalks. I usually walked until 9:00 p.m. but after dark folks weren't so receptive to someone knocking on their front door or ringing the doorbell. I'm sure I interrupted several dinners so during that time I would make my visit quick.

The best walking time was all day Saturday and Sunday afternoons. Even though it was still cold, many folks were outside, raking leaves and generally cleaning up. It's easier to strike up a conversation with someone who is already outside.

Once Betty heard I was walking her precincts, she told her Crime Watch volunteers to keep her informed as to my where-abouts. At least that's what she told newspaper reporters. That was fine. As long as she was doing that she wasn't campaigning herself. I walked Betty's precinct, just like all the others. She returned the favor by leaving one of her brochures on my front door. I didn't get any other indications of Betty walking the district. She probably didn't think she needed to with her vast steering committee of North Dallas Chamber heavies.

One memorable precinct walk encounter went like this. I strode up to the door of a typical ranch style three or four bed room home with lovely, old red oak trees in the front yard and a lawn of lush winter rye grass. I rang the doorbell.

"Whose there?" Came a female voice from inside.

"I'm Jim Richards and I'm a candidate for the Dallas City Council in this area." I was standing up straight and responded with a big smile. "I'd appreciate the opportunity to meet you." I could imagine a sigh from inside, but a woman opened the door anyway.

"Okay, now what do you want young man?"

The lady was probably mid-fifties or so, dressed as if she were about to go to a fancy party.

We shook hands. "Thank you for talking with me. I'm a candidate for District 3 on the Dallas City Council and would appreciate your vote."

"And why should I vote for you? I know Betty Svoboda and work with her in the neighborhood crime watch."

"Well I know Betty too and know she's very active in the program. I'm a businessman. I'm 37 years old and have a 15-year history in the Dallas business community. I've served on a couple of city boards and commissions and worked in the last bond election."

"Okay," she sighed again.

"When was the last time you saw Betty?" I asked.

"Well, I've never actually met her in person. We communicate through the captain of the Crime Watch program in this neighborhood."

I sensed an opening. "Tell me Ma'am, do you have any message for City Hall? What's the most important thing for you in relation to the city?"

"Quit raising the tax rate, fix the potholes and do something about the god-awful traffic congestion."

I had heard all those points before. "You're not the only one with those complaints. I know the tax rate has been increasing and street maintenance has been deferred. I will promise you that when I'm elected, I'll fight for at least three things. Better transportation infrastructure, no new taxes and filling the potholes. I had to replace one of my car's wheel rims because of a pothole so I know what you're talking about."

"I've lived here over 20 years and you're the first candidate for any office to come to my door. I've never even seen a candidate for dog catcher."

"Ma'am, here's a brochure that contains some information about me. When you go to the polls on election day, I hope you'll remember the young man who came to your door."

"I'm going to consider it," she said with enough conviction to convince me that I not only had her vote but the other voters in her household as well and maybe some of her friends.

"Thank you very much," I said while backing down her sidewalk toward the street.

Speaking of dog catchers and dogs, I have a great respect for dogs and many people answered their doors with dog in hand. One day's encounter with a dog was the scariest of all my precinct walks. It made such an impression on me I still remember exactly where it happened. It was in an area bounded by Walnut Hill Lane, Midway Road, Park Lane and Inwood Road. I rang the doorbell, but nothing happened. Thinking maybe the doorbell wasn't working, I decided to try knocking. I heard the deepest, meanest dog bark of my life and then heard the dog racing somewhere that I assumed was toward the door. The collision of the dog with the door was loud and I swear the door bowed out toward me a little. I sprinted down the sidewalk and out to the street as fast as I could. Man's best friend had no intention of being mine that day.

One thing I noticed early on was that folks from each part of the district seem to resemble everyone else in the area. They appeared to be of about the same social-economic level, about the same level of education and were generally interested in the same issues as their neighbors. I presumed that residents of other parts of the City were about the same demographic as their neighbors.

Where I had grown up in Grapeland, a tiny town in East Texas, there was a cross section of humanity. There were good, honest people on the one hand and, on the other hand, like the old oil field saying, there's a thief behind every pine tree in East Texas and there's a lot of pine trees in East Texas. I encountered vastly different levels of education, income, values, social graces and civility. I had probably 25 high school classmates and while no one was rich there were plenty that were poor. I'll never forget two guys in my grade school that didn't have shoes, even in the winter. Their main meal of the day was when the teacher paid 27 cents each for their lunch in the cafeteria. We lived right on the edge of the white community and the "quarters" where the African Americans lived so I was more exposed to racial disparity.

The schools were segregated until the year after I graduated, then the former white elementary school became the elementary school for both blacks and whites, the former black school became the middle school for both blacks and whites and the former white high school became the high school for both blacks and whites. For the first time for either the black or the white schools, Grapeland won the state championship in football.

Some folks, regardless of their socioeconomic status, who grow up in a large urban area, have playmates who are just like them demographically, attend schools with other students who are mostly alike and live in neighborhoods with neighbors who are similar to them. Growing up in Grapeland gave me a bigger picture perspective.

Once I started walking the district, I realized that I was affected by this perspective and the advantage that it allowed me to have. That perspective allowed me to view Dallas, and many other major cities, from the standpoint of the city as a whole. All residents need representation, regardless of their demographic profile. As I listened to the debates among Council members, especially voices of those representing single-member districts, I could understand and appreciate the perspectives of each member's constituents.

Politics should be about bringing people with different ideas together. So often today it's become more about differences, not what we might have in common. It's about differences, but it's not meant to be. Growing up with various types of people and ideas that came together and worked together to solve problems helped me see these possibilities.

FILLING A LEADERSHIP VOID

Five Weeks Till Election Day

Three weeks into the campaign with five weeks to go. I was feeling a little lost and wondering what to do next. The core of the campaign leadership had a meeting at headquarters to "weigh the baby" and try to see where we were. Attending were: David Johnson, Buck Wynne and Bill Booher. All three had good political instincts. During the day there were voter lists strewn about and people milling around but at night it seemed bare. Even though we were all seasoned volunteers, this was the first campaign where we didn't have a professional guiding us, other than Enid helping behind the scenes.

"So where are we and what do we need to do next?" I asked. No one answered but luckily Mike Lindley walked in and took a seat. Mike was an accomplished professional, who came as a volunteer and was one of the good guys. He had been involved in campaigns for years, first as a volunteer and later as a professional and his professionalism showed. He knew we didn't need any cheerleading. What we needed was someone to light a fire.

"You're several weeks into this campaign and only have a little over one month to go. Other than political and civic activists, nobody even knows you're running. He stood up and paced to the small door leading to the headquarters closet sized bathroom. "Yes, you had a press conference but you have to get something out to the voters and quick or you're going down the drain." He took a step into the restroom, leaving the door open so we could hear, and flushed the toilet. "There goes your campaign," he said heading back to his seat.

I looked around the table at the faces of my friends, people who had been working night and day for the past month and were now staring at Mike in stunned silence. "Gee Mike, you sound serious."

One eyebrow shot up as he glared at me. "Hell, you're the one who needs to be serious. You need to get something out to the voters. Who's your campaign chairman?"

"We don't have one yet," I admitted.

"You don't have a chairman? No wonder your campaign has stalled."

"I go out and campaign all day, every day. What else can I do?" I was doing all of the talking from our side, David, Buck and Bill continued to sit and stare at Mike.

"I'll say it again. You need to get something out to the voters. The time for working activists on a wholesale basis is over. Why build up a list of supporters if you don't show it to somebody? Do you have a steering committee?"

I leaned back in my seat, trying to tamp down the churning in my gut.

"We have a great steering committee. It's diversified. We have liberals, conservatives, prochoice, prolife, Democrats, Republicans, Libertarians, and Unitarians. We even have vegetarians."

"You think you're pretty funny don't you?"

"I'm trying to defuse the stress in the room," I said, trying to keep my voice steady despite the tightness in my jaw.

Mike got up. "You need a campaign chair and you need to get a mailer out that includes your steering committee and a campaign chair at the top of the list." He strode out the door. A few of us managed to shoot a quick "Thank you" at his back. Then we sank back into our folding chairs.

"Well, Mike sure knows how to create a sense of urgency." I was having trouble shaking the weight of his words off my shoulders, knowing how difficult recruiting a chair was going to be.

"Trouble is, I've already asked a lot of people who support me, but they don't want the responsibility of chairing a campaign. That job can be an open-ended assignment taking up a lot of time."

Buck had an idea. "We just need a name to go at the top of the list and since our opponent is female it would be helpful if the chairperson were a woman. And why can't we call that person chair of our steering committee?"

I knew he was right. "We have good people working on just about every function and don't need a real campaign chair. I'm filling that function and Buck is acting as a campaign consultant. We need a chair for the name, not to fill a role that's open ended."

We spent the next half hour pouring over the list of names of supporters and debating the merits and probabilities of acceptance for those who had not yet declined. We had to be sensitive about the hard feelings from the bitter 1982 Republican primary battle among Kay Bailey Hutchison, a former state representative from Houston, Jim Jackson, a Dallas County commissioner whose commissioner's district took in a lot of the congressional district and Steve Bartlett, a former Dallas City councilman. Kay and Steve ended up in a runoff and Jim Jackson and his folks supported Steve, who won. Some people say there were some dirty tricks at the end, adding to the hard feelings. The disappointments extended well into 1983. My work on the George H. W. Bush side during the 1980 Presidential primary, earned me an okay guy status. As a result, I was able to pick up several of Kay's supporters for my campaign. Most of them could be classified as moderates. One name stood out above all the rest.

"What about Tory Agnich? She's been a very active moderate Republican and was prominent in Kay's campaign. Her husband is the general counsel of Texas Instruments. Her father-in-law was one of the first Republicans in the Texas Legislature."

Tory was one of at least four of Kay's stalwart workers who helped me with my campaign. Others included Jeanne Johnson, Mary Churchill and Frieda Hudspeth. The four were invaluable in many ways and became not only supporters but friends as well.

Bill finally perked up, leaning forward. "She's perfect. Get with her as soon as you can and ask."

Buck agreed. "There's a citizen meeting about the proposed transit authority at the Hutchison home tonight. Tory is a good friend of Kay and should be there. Get over there and try to persuade her. You should be at that meeting anyway."

I left immediately and headed for the meeting.

Kay's husband, Ray, was greeting folks coming in the door.

"Welcome, come in."

"Ray, I'm Jim Richards. I voted for you in the primary race for governor in 1978 and worked on the phone bank in your campaign."

Ray laughed. "Why thank you very much. You have a good memory. That was five years ago."

I stepped on through the doorway and into the house so Ray could greet other people coming in. I knew a lot of the folks there, but worked the room cautiously, being a Bartlett guy while most of the folks at the meeting were Kay's friends and supporters. I had invited myself to the meeting, so in a way I was a party crasher. I had the feeling you get when you are someplace where you believe you don't belong, like a country boy at a ritzy city event. I carefully avoided Kay. I didn't want to remind her that I was on the other side of the primary battle. Speaking to Ray was enough.

Eventually I spotted Tory Agnich talking to friends in a corner. Tory's pleasing personality appealed to others. She was social and energetic. After her friends moved on to talk to someone else she was left alone so I sat down next to her.

"Hi Tory, I'm Jim Richards."

"I know you, Jim, at least through a lot of mutual friends from the 1980 Bush campaign. They have good things to say about you."

"That's always nice to hear. I hope I'm not intruding but I've got something to ask you. I need some help."

"I'm already on your support list. What else are you looking for?"

"My group has selected you as a campaign chair. You were the overwhelming favorite. In fact, the vote was unanimous."

"Chair your campaign. No way. I don't have time for what would be a very time-consuming job."

Even though I was expecting a negative response, I felt rebuffed. In reality, I couldn't accept "no" for an answer. "I need to get a mailer out to voters. Most of my contacts have been with activists like you. That's gone very well. I'm walking the district but can't possibly reach all the households I need to call on. I need to get out a mailer with my steering committee names on it with yours at the top as chair. Tory, can't you please help out?"

I'm not above groveling when I have to. The stakes are too high to fail.

"Gee, I appreciate your confidence in me, but I have too many obligations right now. I can't chair your campaign. I would be willing to help, though. Any other ideas?"

"How about chairing the steering committee?"

"I could handle that."

"Tory, thank you. You've made my campaign much better." "Well I'm glad to help in a small way."

The meeting was breaking up and guests were leaving Kay and Ray's home. Ray rushed over to me as I was leaving and said "Hey buddy, I heard tonight that you're a candidate for District 3 on the Dallas City Council, but I didn't hear it from you. Any time you enter a room, a home, an event, take advantage of the situation and introduce yourself as a candidate. That way people will know you're running and need some support. It even may just be a matter of them having met you and want to vote for you. Now get out there, run hard and win. And never waste an opportunity to introduce yourself."

"Thanks Ray. That's good advice. Sometimes I need to be reminded."

With that encounter I was out the door. When outside, I lit a cigarette and inhaled some relief. I was self-conscious and had imagined some of the people there staring at me. Judging me, thinking what is that Bartlett guy doing here? It was just my imagination, they didn't care who I was. Ray's comments helped allay those negative feelings.

The last three weeks had been like riding a roller coaster. One minute I was sky high with elation, later that day, down in the dumps because I had missed an opportunity and there was no time left to make it up. The next day, it's top to bottom, bottom to top, then top to bottom again. That whiplash of results can keep one's stomach in a constant churn. It's an adrenaline rush that lasts for days and it's intense, like riding the Comet, the wooden roller coaster at the Texas State Fair.

It's interesting how being involved in a political campaign gave me an excuse to do things I wouldn't normally do. I called strangers on the phone, knocked on stranger's doors. It's okay to pester people about voting on election day, until they either vote or quit answering the phone. It's okay because it's for something larger than one person. It's about a cause. It's okay even when it's your campaign and not a referendum or bond election. The campaign becomes the cause. A campaign is working to elect someone who is conservative, liberal, libertarian, for or against real estate development, and best of all because we believe in putting good people in government who will put their school district, city, state or nation ahead of party or themselves. While I wouldn't normally ask a Tory Agnich to help me in business, it becomes acceptable to do so because it's for a larger cause.

Of all the parts of the campaign, I was proudest of my diverse list of supporters with Tory Agnich on top as chair of the steering committee. The candidate is a vessel to carry the cause, the ideas. It wasn't just Jim Richards, it was all the good people who had signed up, many of whom had a reach in the community far beyond their names alone.

APPROACHING THE MATRIARCH

Four and a Half Weeks Till Election Day

I was early for a meeting with Jack Worley for an update on the campaign. Two walls in his office were covered with aerial photographs of farm land that Jack was trying to buy piece by piece for the company to later sell to some future developer. I'd always been drawn to maps, seeing the big picture of where cities are located in relation to each other. The photographs, being a real-life map, distracted me.

Jack came in and jolted me back to reality. "You have to meet Ebby," He insisted. "She's Betty's campaign fund raiser and you need to get a feel for what you'll be up against. It's a measure of the opponent's strength. Meeting Ebby may be intimidating but this experience will help make Betty less intimidating when you meet her the first time for the first debate."

I protested. "I'm not sure that's what I want to do. It's probably a waste of time. She's never going to help me." *I really mean I don't want to meet her. I've got plenty of time, but I just don't want to go. I can already feel my stomach tighten up.*

"Jim, if nothing else, meeting Ebby is a matter of courtesy and a formal recognition of who she is and what she means to the community. Also, you need to let her know who you are; that you're an okay guy and if you win, you'll be a reasonable Council member, not some erratic young kid. If she thinks you're okay she may not work as hard."

"All right, but I'll have to clear this with Enid first. She's my campaign consultant."

Enid quickly agreed. "Of course, you need to meet Ebby. Call her office and make an appointment. She's probably been wondering who the heck you are and what you're all about. If she likes you at all it might drive a small wedge between her and Betty. I'll get her number and give it to Buck."

The next day I reluctantly called Ebby's office. "Hi, this is Jim Richards. I would like to meet with Ms. Halliday for a few minutes when she can spare the time."

"I check with her if you want to hold."

"Of course," I replied, wondering if I'm ready for this. *This is Ebby Halliday, a civic icon, the most prominent residential realtor in the area and the chair of my opponent's campaign and to her, up until now, I was an unknown.*

From the beginning it felt like I was running against Ebby, since most of the folks I went to see remarked that "Ebby has already been here" or "Ebby called the other day about Betty." Of course, if Ebby were the candidate I wouldn't be in the race. She, like Wayne Callaway at Frito Lay, had a business to run and civic issues to address.

After a minute or so she returned with, "How about this afternoon in her office at 2:00 p.m.?"

"Tell her I'll be there at two o'clock sharp." *I'm not ready to go. What am I going to say to her? What will she say to me? Why did I ever agree to do this?*

I fretted about Ebby's response to me. While I didn't know Betty, I had a great deal of respect for her, or who she was and all she had accomplished. However, the reality was that Ebby seemed like the opposition to me even though her name won't be on the ballot. Many people supporting Betty attributed their support to Ebby. Meeting with her would be like meeting with Betty. Anything thing I said wrong could be used against me.

I ran into Jack Worley later that morning. "I'm going to see Ebby this afternoon. What should I tell her?"

"Just be yourself. Treat her like you would any other opinion leader. She isn't ever going to support you, but you need to be sure of yourself. Walk into her office with confidence; tell her you know she's supporting Betty. Tell her who you are and about yourself and ask for her support. She will have more respect for you if you do that. When you win, you don't want her as an adversary. You have nothing to lose and everything to gain."

Yeah, I have a lot to lose. What if I go in there and choke? That would be the ultimate embarrassment. She would tell Betty and Betty would find a way or venue to use it against me. I better be ready because if I try to bluff my way in she will see through it in a heartbeat.

Two o'clock came quickly, and I set out to meet Ebby. Her office was not the iconic former Preston Hollow City Hall at the northwest corner of Preston Road and Northwest Highway, that was one of her many sales offices. The headquarters was nearby in a two-story brick building in Preston Center. As I walked up the stairs to her second floor office my stomach churned. Jack had framed it as a reconnaissance mission. See what the enemy is like. Assess your opponent. I hadn't met Betty or Ebby before today and thought I needed to get an idea of what they were thinking.

I reached the top of the stairs and went inside a rather unpretentious office suite. It was an office of someone who had nothing to prove. Nicely decorated, but I guess it wasn't how I pictured the office of someone as successful and famous as Ebby Halliday. Facing the receptionist, I was now behind enemy lines. I put on a brave front.

"Hello, I have an appointment with Ms. Halliday at two o'clock."

"And your name is?"

"Jim Richards."

"Ah, Jim Richards. I've heard a lot about you. I'll tell her you're here." She went into a private office and after a few seconds emerged. "You can come in and see her now."

There I was standing before the revered Ebby Halliday. "Hello Ms. Halliday," I said as I extended a handshake. "I'm Jim Richards and it's a real pleasure. I've been wanting to meet you long before this campaign began but didn't think it would be under these circumstances."

Ebby was courteous. "Have a seat and tell me why you're here."

Her welcome helped me relax. Meeting Ebby in person wasn't as intimidating as I thought it would be. She wasn't ten feet tall after all. "Ms. Halliday, you've been very busy. As you know, I'm running for the City Council. Practically everyone I've called on said 'Ebby has already been here or Ebby called me the other day about supporting Betty'. I know you're supporting Betty but wanted to tell you who I am and why I'm running."

"Go right ahead." I could tell she was sizing me up as Betty's opponent, and I could feel some apprehension, not based on anything she said or did but just my gut reaction. Despite Ebby's gracious manner and my giving her the respect she deserved, there was a lot of tension and conflict with both of us beneath the surface.

"I'm 37 years old and have a 15-year record in the business world. I spent 10 years as a CPA with Deliotte Haskins & Sells and 5 years with Gulf United Corporation doing mergers and acquisitions. I've served on the board of the Dallas County Community Action Committee and on the Dallas Civil Service Board. I worked as a volunteer in the last City bond election. I had wanted to leave East Texas and live in Dallas for as long as I can remember. I love the city and want to give something back. I believe in balanced growth, especially with improved transportation systems. I want to do something about the traffic gridlock here. I know you are supporting Betty, but I would like your support for me too."

Ebby hesitated for a few seconds then leaned back in her chair, staring at me over her glasses, and said, "Well, I wondered who you really were and what you were all about." She shrugged and smiled. "You know I can't support you and we're going to beat you on election day. Thanks for coming by."

With that dismissal, she picked up a pen and went back to work.

I stood and said. "Thank you for taking the time to see me. I hope the next time we meet we'll be on the same side."

I left the room, exhaled in relief that the meeting I dreaded was over. I walked down to the bottom of the stairs and out of the building. One more step in the campaign was behind me. Boy, a stiff drink would be good right now, maybe a double scotch on the rocks or a dry martini.

The meeting with Ebby gave me a gage of where we were with the campaign. If they didn't perceive me as a threat, I wouldn't have been invited to her office. She was probably as eager to meet me as Jack and Enid were insistent that I see her.

When I returned to campaign headquarters, Buck met me at the door. Ruth stood within earshot waiting to hear the result of my meeting with Ebby.

"Okay, how did it go?"

"Ebby was extremely nice to me and the gracious host that I expected. I learned that they're confident about winning and it will be a pretty big shock to them if I win."

"It's good that they're over confident. And remember, it's not if but when you win. You can't let losing be any part of your makeup."

Meeting Ebby was one of the last few wholesale political connections to make. There were a few others but meeting people and asking for their vote seemed much more directly tied to winning and losing. How did it help the campaign? I didn't want Ebby as an enemy whether I won or lost. Having met me in person she knew I wasn't some cocky kid that would do something radical at City Hall. Maybe, just maybe, she will decide that she's done enough for Betty and will ease up for the rest of the campaign. In any event, it was an experience that added to my growth as a candidate and a person. I've always felt that way about meeting folks of her stature.

In parting I announced to those in the office, "I'm glad I went. I'm going to grab a walk list and go knock on doors and shake some hands." I enjoyed walking from house to house and was always curious who would answer the door and how I would be received. The overwhelming majority appreciated an actual candidate coming to their door to meet them in person and listen to their concerns with city government.

IT'S ABOUT MONEY AND FUNCTIONS

Four Weeks Till Election Day

Most campaigns have their usual ups and downs, and mine was no different. Money was slow coming in. My first finance chair and good friend, Rex Jobe, warned me that he had to concentrate on his business about the time I started running. Our office was one floor down from Gulf United's offices at Preston Road and the LBJ Freeway. Bo West, my immediate boss had leased space as part of a tax move for him and a few other executives and their operation was finished. They rented it to us month to month.

Sally McKenzie, a force in the George H.W. Bush wing of the Republican Party, appeared in the campaign office one day. Sally and her husband Bill, a former GOP county chairman, had been in charge of Bush's presidential campaign in Dallas County and thereabouts.

Sally and her family lived in Highland Park, an inner-city suburb with plenty of old money to go around. Sally was pure old Highland Park, in terms of grace, but without pretense. I liked and respected Sally. I had worked under her leadership in the 1980 Republican presidential primary on the side of George H.W. Bush, who was pitted against the more conservative Ronald Reagan. I was a grass roots precinct organizer and a regional legislative district chair of the precinct organization. I recruited precinct captains for each precinct and led their efforts to organize on the precinct level. After Reagan won, he picked Bush as his running mate in an attempt to unite the party and of course, bring in Texas oil and gas money. Most of the Bush people never quit working after the primary. We just worked for the Reagan-Bush combined ticket.

Today, Sally was all business. "Okay, where are you with finances? How much money do you have and how much do you need to finish the campaign?"

"I don't know how much we need. The first reporting about

contributions shows us way behind. Betty's raised $23,942 but she's been collecting since June of last year. The report shows us at $8,237. If you count what we've raised since the reporting period ended it's about $15,000 and we've spent all of it. Everyone says we need to redesign the brochure and do another mailing. We could end up needing another $50,000 before the campaign is over."

"Where is that coming from?" Sally asked.

"Damned if I know. I've been busy electioneering and haven't worked much on the finances. When I call on a potential donor, I always leave a pledge card and ask for their support. Donations are coming in but not anything significant. It's almost like they're hedging their bets on Ebby, I mean on Betty."

"You need more help. I'm going to see John Massey in his office upstairs at Gulf United. He's a Democrat. He's on the board of directors of M Bank and knows many of the heavy weights in this town."

"Thanks Sally." Sally seemed to know everyone that was anyone in Highland Park and was apparently friends with John's wife.

Sally went upstairs to talk to John about fundraising. After about a half hour she returned with a report. She gave me a blow by blow.

"I told John your campaign was going well. We believe you have a real future in politics and can win this race for City Council. I told him you needed help with fund raising."

She continued with the details. "He promised to contact either Jess Hay or Ted Enloe to help." They were the chairman and president, respectfully of Lomas and Nettleton Financial Corporation, one of the largest mortgage banks in the country and both were prolific fund raisers for Democratic candidates. I thanked Sally as she was leaving and walked her out to the elevator.

Over the next few weeks the money started rolling in and continued. I even got a check from Ben Barnes, a charismatic former Democrat elected official with an appearance made for television.

Ben went on to become Speaker of the Texas House of Representatives, one of the most powerful positions in Texas government. He later became lieutenant governor, the most powerful position. In Texas, the governor has more political power but the lieutenant- governor has more constitutional power as the leader of the State Senate. There is a tradition of members in the State House and Senate to cede power in the House to the speaker and power in the Senate to the lieutenant-governor to maximize the work they can get done during the January to May biennial session and avoid special sessions.

Many saw Ben as a future president of the United States. Unfortunately, his rise was side tracked by a handful of bank scandals, which sent a few folks, close to him, to jail. Ben had done nothing wrong, but his name was associated with others around him who were convicted. The general population and of course jury pools were mad as hell.

While Ted Enloe, who was an active fund raiser, was hitting the Democratic contributors, Sally worked a few of the old time Republicans. One of her good friends sent me a $1,000 check, the maximum contribution one could make. Several folks in the real estate industry contributed, again probably as a hedge, in case I won.

Sometimes, offhand conversations can lead to much larger things down the road. I was updating Steve Bartlett on my progress. "Call Andy Clendenen. You can get his number from my campaign office."

Andy ran a five-location restaurant group called "Andrews", where it seemed like a third of the people I knew either met their eventual spouse or proposed to them in one of his popular restaurants. It must have been something in the water, or maybe in the drinks.

The next day I called Andy the first chance I got "Andy, I'm Jim Richards."

"And who are you?"

"I'm a candidate for the Dallas City Council District 3, where you live. Steve Bartlett recommended that I call you. I need your help and support."

"Sure, if Bartlett says you're okay, you're okay with me. I'm happy to support you."

"I've been to most, if not all, of your restaurants. Love your jalapeno hamburgers."

"Well thanks for your business. If you see me there, introduce yourself."

"Thanks for your support, Andy. I really appreciate it."

I sent Andy a pledge card and a couple of days later a check showed up in the mail. About ten years later Andy and I met in person and became good friends and partners in a couple of business ventures.

I kept thinking more about the cause and the campaign. I started to see myself as a cog in the wheels of a larger phenomenon. The checks coming in were one more example of how this campaign was important to a lot of people. What did the community want? I believed it was electing someone to City Hall who listened to what people said rather than telling them what to do. The citizens of Dallas wanted someone in City Hall who would bring together people with different opinions and positions and achieve a compromise. It was about electing someone who would work behind the scenes to achieve solutions, rather than talk and complain about them in public. It was a good cause and I was just a vessel to carry it in.

In the investment banking business, the quality of a transaction can be more important than the persuasiveness of the person selling the transaction. The same is true for fund raising for a political campaign. If the cause is important enough, money will come in. If it's not, money won't be there.

I was at our headquarters one day, signing thank you letters and reveling over the checks that were coming in. Buck came to work later that day after a session at law school, bringing with him instructions from Enid.

"This campaign needs an event, something where people can meet you and hear you out. There have been a few neighborhood coffees, but this would be an opportunity to raise more money and create more excitement in the race. Let's have a 6:00 p.m. reception at the Weston Hotel in the Galleria. Not a fund raiser, per say, but an event. A pledge/donation card will be included in the invitation for anyone who wants to give, even a small amount."

Bill Booher, the campaign treasurer, stopped by after work and helped with the planning of the event. "If someone puts as little as one dollar into a campaign, they have skin in the game. They have a stake in the outcome and will not only vote but will suggest you to others."

"Who do we invite?" I asked.

"Everybody on your support list, everybody who is on the both the mayor's and Betty's lists of contributors (it was public information).

Bill added. "And anyone else who we might think could be helpful."

Buck went on. "Whatever we do we don't want a large room that doesn't fill up. Nothing creates excitement about a candidate as an overcrowded room. We'll serve coffee and cookies. "We all agreed that a room of about 1,000 square feet would work, hoping we could fill it."

The evening of the event the room started filling up. Several folks arrived who had business before the Council, notably Willie Cothrum, a former Council member who served as a consultant to developers who wanted zoning changed and his partner, Joe Barta, whose wife Carolyn was a political columnist for the *Dallas Morning News* and one of my favorite journalists.

By 6:30 the room was packed. The crowd overflowed into the hall outside. Buck and Bill came over to me.

Buck said, "It's time for a speech. They want to hear something. Stand on a chair in the middle of the room and turn around as you speak, making sure you project to everyone." He jested, "don't go so fast as to get dizzy, though."

This was the first campaign function of its type and there was an opportunity here in this room to reach people who hadn't paid much attention to the campaign. This race included more fireworks than all of the other Council races combined and the media's attention to the race had made many folks aware of it.

I was uplifted by the crowd and without hesitation or thought of the consequences of falling; I hopped up onto a chair. Luckily, the chair didn't overturn and send me sailing into the crowd. I commenced to give my standard pitch about neighborhoods, planned growth, and transportation and, of course, no new taxes. My standard pitch was well received.

I had another function to go to, a neighborhood get together, at seven o'clock.

Buck said, "Get out of here now. You don't want to be here when the last person leaves. Apologize to the crowd and be on your way."

"Friends and neighbors, I have to run out and go to another function. Thank you again for coming and I'm looking forward to working with all of you after the election."

I shook as many hands as I could on the way out and was quickly on my way to the next function. The reception felt good with so many people there, even the ones who came to hedge their bets.

The next function was one arranged by Harvey Williams. A friend of Harvey's hosted a coffee for me at his home.

I arrived and worked the room for the requisite half hour.

The sponsor wanted to get the show going so he introduced me, and I repeated the speech that I gave earlier at the reception. I stayed as long as people were there since there was nothing else on my schedule. As I was leaving, an attractive, middle-aged woman walked in. She wore a look of determination on her face.

"Where's the candidate?" she demanded. "I want to meet him before he leaves. I hope he's still here."

Music to my ears. "Hi, I'm Jim Richards, the candidate and it's a pleasure to meet you."

"Whew," she said. Then raised her voice so everyone left in the house could hear. "I just came from another function and had some exposure to your opponent. I wanted to meet you. After meeting her I knew I was going to vote for you if you weren't a yellow dog."

A yellow dog is an old Texas political term coming from the nickname, Yellow Dog Democrat, describing someone who would vote Democrat, even if a yellow dog was running. Her use of it was strictly non-partisan. The implication is that a yellow dog must be fairly low on the scale of mammals, including humans, but who am I to say, being no judge of canines myself.

The compliment, even if it was something about not being a yellow dog, was encouraging and gave me an emotional lift. "I'm really glad I got to meet you. Even though your criteria are fairly low, I hope I did pass it."

She laughed loudly. "You even have a sense of humor. I'm telling my friends on this side of town that we have an option on election day. We don't have to vote for Betty." I kept remembering my telephone conversation with Betty and her attempts to intimidate me into not running.

Even though there were ups and downs, each step the last few days, the checks, the success of the function and now the lady at the coffee, added to my confidence that this race was winnable.

Another word about raising money. Phil and Diana Cobb lived in the Bluffview neighborhood. Diana was active in civic affairs, primarily with neighborhood preservation issues. Phil was a cofounder of "The Black-Eyed Pea," a chain of restaurants that specialized in home-style cooking. Bluffview was and still is a quaint neighborhood full of twisting, crooked streets, hills and many huge old trees. It can be tricky to drive through unless you know your way around. There is hardly any cut through traffic, a country feel within the city. As a result, it's a quiet and peaceful place and folks who live there want to keep it that way.

As so many things seemed to start in this campaign, my phone rang. It was Enid. "Phil Cobb and his wife want to host a function for you. They'll open up the Black-Eyed Pea on Forest Lane on a Sunday afternoon ten days from now. That will give us time to mail invitations. The opening is 2-4:00 p.m. between their lunch and dinner crowds."

"That's wonderful news. I believe we should have it like the one in the Weston." I had learned something from the Weston reception. "No donation will be required but the invitation will include a pledge/donation card to give those invited to either endorse me and/or make a contribution. They can mail it back or bring it to the function. Let's also have plenty of yard signs and bumper stickers as well as extra brochures and pledge cards."

"You should serve light hors d'oeuvres, coffee, tea and wine. I won't be there but Buck will represent me," Enid instructed.

The function started early. Folks began arriving at 1:45, even while the lunch crowd was thinning out. We officially opened up at two o'clock sharp and I stood by the door to welcome everyone and thank them for coming. By 2:45 the place was full. Buck took charge. "Okay, you have greeted everyone, now go back and work the room until 3:15. Then it will be speech time. Do you know what you are going to say?"

"I'll thank everyone for coming, comment on how great the turnout was, talk about issues and end with time for questions."

Lisa Saeman was there working the room as well. She came over with Buck to move me to the next duty. "How about saying, 'I won't raise taxes unless it's absolutely necessary.' That gives you a back door if something happens."

"Problem is how do you know when it's absolutely necessary?"

Lisa sighed and gave a half-hearted shrug. "Okay, no new taxes."

A few years later Lisa ran for the City Council. One of her campaign promises was no new taxes unless it's absolutely necessary. I tried for the no new taxes period, but she was the candidate that time and finally got her way.

I worked the room until Buck and Lisa called on me to speak. I gave my usual speech that ended with my no new taxes slogan.

An older man I didn't recognize in the back of the room raised his hand with a question and his tone was laced with sarcasm. "What happens, Mr. Richards, if the city has a real need for additional revenue? How can you make such an air tight pledge?"

I suspected he was a plant from Betty's campaign. "Thank you for the question, Sir. It's a good one."

He spoke again and was quite the smart mouth. "Yes, it's a good question and that's why I asked it. Why don't you answer it?"

I nodded to the guy and looked directly into his eyes, then turned to the rest of the folks to reply. "Our city is rapidly expanding its tax base because of all the new commercial real estate development. While we need to keep that development out of the neighborhoods, there are plenty of places to build and with new construction the tax base grows.

There is no senior citizen exemption or homestead exemption on commercial real estate, so as the commercial real estate part of the tax base grows, tax revenues grow proportionally. We can make lots of improvements without raising the tax rate."

Several folks in the audience murmured their approval.

The man in the back spoke up again in an apparent attempt to have me pledge something I would regret either way. He wanted to box me in. "Is your position that you will not vote to raise taxes under any circumstances or something softer like you will not vote to raise taxes unless it's absolutely necessary?"

"I'm saying no tax increase. Saying something like unless it's absolutely necessary would give me an out. Absolutely necessary is a subjective term. What's absolutely necessary to you may not be absolutely necessary to someone else."

The erstwhile heckler wouldn't give up. "But what if there is a disaster and taxes must be raised to bail the city out of a crisis."

"I love our former Cowboy quarterback Dandy Don Meredith saying on the Monday Night Football broadcast if ifs and buts were candy and nuts, we would all have a Merry Christmas." Most everyone in the crowd laughed.

I continued. "The people of this city are wise. If there's is a reason to bail this city out of a crisis I'll go to the people and tell them that circumstances have changed and we will explore and determine the best course of action."

With that the crowd started clapping, as if they didn't want to hear the guy in the back say anything else. Buck stood up on a chair. "Thanks to everyone for coming. It's time to start clearing out so this Black-Eyed Pea can get ready for the dinner crowd."

Well, I believe I got through that exchange unscathed and this function seems to have been a success. Onward and upward!

As the place cleared out I said good bye to each person and thanked them again for coming. When they were all gone Buck, Lisa and I sat down at the bar for a beer.

"We ended on a very positive note," Buck said after his first sip of beer.

"I am opposed to any new taxes whatsoever from now to the end of time," Lisa joked.

"Lisa, you have to run yourself. You will make a great candidate."

"I'll be your campaign manager, even if I'm still in law school," Buck said.

Even though it was my campaign, we all felt like comrades working on a larger cause. Being in those circumstances brings people together in a good way.

One fundraiser that I attended wasn't given for me and didn't raise money directly for me but played a significant role in the campaign. Many of the events that candidates attended included the candidates for each single-member district as well as the candidates for the two at-large seats. During these stops I got to know Annette Strauss, who was running for one of the at-large or citywide open seats. She and I became friends, which would make a difference to both of us down the line.

Sid Stahl was an invaluable ally, helping put together an ad in a Jewish weekly newspaper. He also convinced Annette into letting me attend one of her fund raiser events. With the host's permission, I attended a large private event in Leon and Idelle Rabin's townhouse at Royal Lane and the Dallas North Tollway. Annette and I moved among the guests and introduced ourselves. Annette spoke to the group first and then it was my turn.

Sid introduced me. "This man, Jim Richards, will make a good councilman. He's smart and he's a moderate, especially compared to his opponent who can be too conservative and too outspoken. I haven't heard this, but it's been said that she's made anti-Semitic remarks. With that there were a few nods and other signs of agreement. I didn't know if they had heard it before or if they were just assuming that she would do that.

I gave my usual campaign pitch but didn't mention my no new taxes stand. I did, however, mention support for the arts. After the event, endorsements and dollars from those in attendance came in for several weeks thereafter.

Jetta attended a few of the functions and events with me but usually stuck to her English riding hobby with an organization called the "Hickory Creek Hunt". Both Jetta and I were gone from home a lot during the two-month campaign but Victoria, our Au Pair from Switzerland, was there to help with our son Murk. Murk loved Victoria.

Jetta and I had different interests that we pursued in our spare time so the campaign really didn't affect our relationship. I dropped everything I used to do on my own and replaced it with the campaign. Jetta pursued her hobby when she wasn't involved in the campaign.

Working on these functions was satisfying. It was the collective efforts of many good, hard working people committed to a cause. The volunteers make the campaign. By running, I realized how powerful I and other volunteers had been in the various things we worked on. The race may be more exciting to the candidate, but volunteering makes one as much a part of the cause as the candidate.

BUILDING MOMENTUM

Three Weeks Till Election Day

I was walking door to door one Saturday morning late in the campaign. I didn't think about bringing an umbrella until the rain became more of a shower than a drizzle. The winter temperatures and rain made the walk miserable. I didn't care. Saturday was always a productive walking day since most people were at home in the morning, especially when inclement weather limited most outdoor activities.

One mid-afternoon, I had just finished my last house call when Buck pulled up to the curb, rolled down his car window and shouted. "I've been looking for you. Ruth gave me the precinct location where you'd be walking. I knew you were going to win when I saw you out there walking in the rain. Damn you're determined. I've got great news. The *Dallas Times Herald* has endorsed you."

The *Times Herald* was one of Dallas' two newspapers and gave more focus to local news than its competitor, the *Dallas Morning News*.

"That's great! My interview with Ron Calhoun, a political columnist, was a couple of days ago. He usually covers partisan races and gave no indication as to which way they were leaning."

Since I had finished my walk for the day I was ready to celebrate, to go someplace warm and dry. Back at headquarters we showed the editorial to Ruth, the campaign office manager. "I'm thrilled. We're going to win this election. I can feel it in my bones."

Buck called Enid after she was finished at the Taylor campaign headquarters. "I told her to meet us at the Weekly Gray McKinney office for a celebration when she finished. I have keys and it's six o'clock already, let's go on over."

We grabbed a six pack of beer and headed to Enid's McKinney

Avenue office.

Enid came through the door and took in the sight of the two of us, leaned back in our chairs with a half empty beer in our hands. "Ok boys, it's good that you got the *Times Herald*. It's good that you got the Police and Fire Association. Betty has been campaigning since mid-June and now it's late February. Do you think she's going to just give up and concede, three weeks before the election?"

Buck put his beer down. "Well, she might as well because we're getting all of the endorsements."

Enid shot back. "Did you get the Realtors Association? Did you get the Real Estate Developers Association? Did you get all of the leadership in the North Dallas Chamber of Commerce?"

"We didn't expect those," I said. Betty only got those endorsements because of Ebby."

"Oh, so you think they won't count, huh." Enid retorted. "Here's what you should expect. You think your opponent is down and out. You think they have been put away. You relax. You have a celebration, like you're doing now! They may lay low for a day or two to gather themselves, and then they'll come out swinging hard. Look for something negative. Their strategy has been to more or less ignore you since you announced, thinking the campaign was over and their best avenue was to say nothing. The *Times Herald* and police and fire have awakened them. They are startled and know a comeback push is necessary."

Enid was right. She was a veteran of many campaigns. It wasn't long before they threw the counterpunch. They had too much of an investment in the effort not to come back swinging hard.

Tom James, a Dallas attorney active in the North Dallas Chamber and in Republican politics supported Betty. I'd never met him nor spoken to him on the phone. The *Dallas Morning News* had started covering the race more closely, since signs were it was now a heated race. They interviewed Tom about the race and his evaluation of Betty and me. Nobody would remember anything about the article except the last thing that Tom said, "Betty's tough, this guy Richards isn't. He's Milquetoast, that's all. That's not who we need representing North Dallas."

Well, it was like a movie scene where a bad guy has been shot, beat half to death or worse and is left for dead or at least unconscious. The good guys are relieved that the fight is over and turn their backs on the bad guy. Suddenly, the bad guy springs to life and attacks again. Not only has our opponent sprung back to life but they are hitting below the belt.

I wasn't prepared for a personal attack but I was going to have to deal with it because I knew more attacks were coming. The milquetoast comment was like that, a dirty punch. Campaigns in those days consisted of discussing qualifications and issues. A personal attack like this in a non-partisan race was rare. There was usually more courtesy among candidates than contention, especially in a municipal race.

Was I qualified? Was I tough enough? This tapped into a doubt I had from the beginning; why me? Why should I be the one to take on Betty and her henchmen when there were people who were smarter, better connected and could raise more money? Was I fearless or just naive enough to try it?

I knew I needed to respond, but how? "Buck, Enid warned us about this and now it's happened. What's our next move? I have to respond and respond in a way so that I don't come across as milquetoast or as a cry baby. I need to hit back hard, not once but twice."

The *Dallas Morning News* must have believed that this race had become a story. They loved a back and forth and called me later that night for a response.

I was ready for the call. "As a corporate executive, I'm involved in management, including hiring and firing people. Betty is a realtor and shows houses to buyers. She isn't involved in management, doesn't handle or solve personnel problems, much less hire or fire people. It's a serious undertaking, not as pleasant as showing a house."

The story played well in the News the next day, appearing on the front page of the Metro section.

"Well, I can kiss the realtors goodbye after that comment," I told Buck later that day.

"Yeah, but many of those realtors are competitors of Ebby and Betty, and you know Betty has insulted more than a few people over the years."

"Now there is a debate to prepare for. A neighborhood association in Northwest Dallas is having a debate tonight. It's a candidate forum for the two at-large Council races and District 3; you and Betty. A good showing there should help to offset the negative effects of the newspaper article, you know, the milquetoast comment."

By now my nerves were on edge. "Alright Buck, whose side are you on? You don't need to remind me, don't need to keep repeating 'milquetoast'. Tonight's so-called debate is a candidate forum. Since it's not a formal debate, there isn't much preparation to do. I know what the issues are. Neither one of us has been a Council member so the forum is just an opportunity to talk about qualifications, why we're running and to separate ourselves from the other candidate."

That night the candidate forum was in a mid-sized room in a neighborhood recreation center. It was a typical bare room without anything other than a few chairs. The room was crowded, which meant that the newspaper exposure had created more interest than usual. This was my first time to experience Betty face to face. We had never even been in the same building at the same time.

The room was full of voting age citizens, actually a lot of senior citizens, who were more inclined to vote in any election than younger voters. The candidates in the at-large candidate's races went first, giving them an opportunity to leave for other commitments of a city-wide campaign.

About nine o'clock it was our turn. After a short break, the forum moderator called the meeting back to order.

"Thanks everyone for staying for this last debate. I see that Betty Svoboda is here, Betty, please lead off."

"As most of you know, I run the Neighborhood Crime Watch organization for most of Northwest Dallas. I know the area well. I've been on the board of the North Dallas Chamber of Commerce, so I'm connected to the business community here. Finally, I'm a former member of the Dallas Park Board, which controls all the pools and recreation centers, Fair Park and several other import- ant city facilities. The Park Board makes all these decisions, from buying grass mowers to hiring the director." Then she finished with, "It's a more important organization and experience than serving on the Civil Service Board like Jim has, debating the details of civil service rules."

Betty was glaring at me when she made the last comment, as if she needed to emphasize something. Betty was a smart, hard working person and I never knew if she sincerely disliked me or just wanted to win and was beginning to see me as a threat. Everyone in the room turned and starred at me, waiting on a retort.

Boy, that woman had a talent for belittling a person. I couldn't leave the milquetoast comment hanging out there unanswered. I had to hit back. I had been insulted again and had enough. I dramatically removed my suit coat and handed it to Buck, then loosened my tie. The room fell silent, everyone sensed a fight was coming. The moderator turned to me. "You must be the other candidate in the race" knowing full well who I was from Betty's glaring look at me. *Well, yes it's me.*

I stepped forward, put on a little East Texas and proudly started with "Why yes I am. Thank you all for corning and your interest in municipal affairs. I'm Jim Richards, a 37-year-old business man with a 15 year background in the business world. I'm a CPA and have worked in public accounting with Deloitte Haskins & Sells for 10 years and with a local investment company for another five as vice president-corporate planning, which means I work on growing the company with acquisitions."

"Betty, you've bragged on yourself but said nothing about what you would do if you were elected. I will. I want to protect our neighborhoods from overdevelopment and traffic problems and I will make this pledge; no new taxes, period."

Speaking directly to Betty, "Betty, the Civil Service Board does a lot more than oversee rule changes, which, by the way, are important to employees, citizens and tax payers. Ask any of the thousands of city employees, especially firefighters and police officers. Ask them if those rules protect them from bureaucratic indifference."

I felt the adrenaline rush as I pictured myself on the Merry-Go-Round that Skip Pedlar had described earlier. I could see the brass ring coming up and reached out to grab it.

I continued. "In addition to overseeing changes in civil service rules, a member of our board sits on three-member trial boards with two City Council members; the trial boards hear appeals from employees who have been terminated and want to appeal their termination. Betty, think about sitting on a trial board of a terminated police officer with a previously impeccable eighteen-year record who allegedly shot a suspect in the back fleeing from the scene of a crime. His employment has been terminated by the chief and he is appealing that decision. Compare handling that situation with approving the purchase of a lawn mower." *Take that, says the milquetoast. You left yourself open by mentioning purchase of lawnmowers.*

Each time I called her out, she scowled and started to respond. With that last remark and before Betty had a chance for a retort the moderator announced, "You have both had a chance to speak. We're way over the time granted us to use the building. We must clear the room now and exit the building immediately," thus ending the forum. He quickly thanked all the candidates who were still there and all the attendees, which were about forty to fifty people, fewer by far than the number of folks who had seen the newspaper article, but it was a start.

Buck grabbed my arm. "Hey Milquetoast, that was a good ending and she didn't have a chance to respond. It's after nine, let's go to Joe's where all the reporters hang out and have a beer."

"Let's do that. I'm ready for a celebration." I called Jetta when we got to Joe's but she, Murk and Victoria were enjoying themselves with a late dinner at home. I was disappointed she couldn't join us.

Politics is often viewed as an abstract machine that rolls along in an impersonal way. My reaction to the milquetoast comment is a good example of how politics often affects candidates and office-holders on a personal level. Everyone who runs for office is vulnerable to criticism. That vulnerability may discourage folks from running. However, we need more good people to try it. Some of the best advice I got, and it came from several sources, is to stick to the issues and never attack or criticize someone on a personal level. Always make it about the issues, never about them personally.

Being confronted with the milquetoast comment made me realize how the nature of this race had changed from discussing the issues to personal insults. I reeled from the comment, taking it personally instead of realizing that Tom didn't know me, and someone probably urged him to say it for the campaign. Once I accepted that it didn't smart as much.

Several supporters came to me urging me to strike back against the milquetoast comment. Fred Stem was first. Fred was a savvy guy who had a recommendation.

"What you need is called a negative drop. A brochure consisting of a wide page with positive things about you on the left side and negative things about your opponent on the right side, allowing someone to sum things up at a glance. Then you drop it on doorsteps during the last few days of the campaign when they don't have time to answer it."

I was hesitant, since going negative can backfire. "Gee, this sounds like a dirty trick. Besides, it's too early to even think about it. Election Day is two weeks away at this point and I hate to go negative, even if they are. Win or lose, I have to live in this town and want to have good relations with folks on the other side. Let them take the low road. I will agree to think about it, but I doubt that I'll want to do it."

I had previously told the newspapers about my experience as a businessman and contrasted that with Betty's experience as a realtor. They quickly retaliated with a letter from Ebby to the *Dallas Morning News* that they also mailed to voters in the district. Ebby used the terms "shocked and dismayed" by my comments. She also questioned my honesty saying that I had been "less than forthright" about the fact that through subsidiaries Gulf United owned land in Far North Dallas and one of its other subsidiaries was Republic National Life Insurance Company, which was negotiating a problem with the City regarding group insurance.

When asked by reporters about the letter, I called the mailer a "dirty trick" and a "desperation tactic," that the land was only 15 acres in Far North Dallas that would probably be condemned when the Dallas North Tollway was extended. Besides, I had no authority over Republic National Life, which was acquired by Gulf United long after the problem arose. Furthermore, unlike Ms. Halliday's firm, Gulf United was a publicly held corporation that makes full disclosures on a quarterly basis.

The next day Paula Stringer, who was one of Ebby Halliday's biggest rivals, called my campaign office and gave a verbal endorsement, and said her check to my campaign was in the mail.

I called her back the minute I found out. "Ms. Stringer, thank you so very much. I really appreciate your endorsement and it couldn't have come at a better time."

"Just call me Paula, and we are going to beat Ebby, aren't we?"

I was glad I was running against Betty and not Ebby but replied, "Yes, we are going to beat Ebby and Betty."

At a meeting one day at our now busy and active headquarters David began by stressing the power of media.

"Don't underestimate the importance of media in a political campaign. The media can have a tremendous impact on the outcome of an election. The effect usually comes from reporters covering the story. Their narratives can be subtle but highly influential. If the news media reports something about a candidate, it's more believable than statements directly from a candidate or their opponent."

In those days' people generally believed what they read in the newspaper or heard on the TV or radio. This is in contrast with today's era of "Post Truth," where facts are less influential in shaping public opinion than appeals to emotion and personal beliefs.

"Of course, the media is important. "What do I need to do?"

"You need to make yourself available to the media. Before any interaction with the media, think about what points you want to make and whether it's a formal interview or just a casual question, concentrate on how to work in your points, regardless of the question."

"You're right. The media can be more powerful than paid advertising. I've got it," I said to David as he left for work.

There were several other sources, many of whom worked for other candidates. Tony Garrett, a former radio reporter, was the media consultant for Jerry Rucker's campaign for the City Council. Jerry, the owner of a construction company, was running for one of the at-large places and had the backing of the real estate community. Tony and I became friends on the campaign trail. He gave me one of my most repeated sayings to others, be they politicians, bureaucrats or whatever. Tony's advice to me was that "nothing is ever, ever, ever, off the record. A reporter's job is to get stories and report the news. That's what they get paid to do, not to listen to your problems, not advise or help candidates in any way."

David called me the next day at the campaign office before I started my afternoon and evening precinct walks. His points were similar to Fred's. "Jim, you have to strike another blow soon. Time is running out and you've probably made many realtors and their friends and families angry. That milquetoast comment really put us on our heels. You had a good response, but the voters heard his description first. I know you're methodically walking the precincts in the district and meeting voters one on one and Betty isn't, but still, we need to do something bigger than your retail campaign. Meeting voters one at a time won't get the job done. You need to go wholesale and create a splash that will be on the news and reach a lot of voters. "I have an idea. Several other folks have suggested the same thing. You need to come out and publicly call Betty a 'North Dallas Elsie Faye Higgins.' "

Elsie Faye Higgins, a well-known African-American civil rights activist, was elected in 1980 to represent South Dallas (District 6) on the City Council. She was one of the first, but surely not the last, to be elected without ties to the white establishment who had a great deal of influence in city politics. Elsie Faye had a booming voice and was almost always on the local 10:00 p.m. news for speaking for or against something. If you watched the local TV news or read either Dallas newspaper, you knew who Elsie Faye Higgins was, no matter where you lived. She had a real knack for being in front of the cameras.

I laughed at the thought but declined. "No. That would be a dirty trick and a personal attack. Let them be the ones with the personal attacks. Besides, if I win, I will need to work with Elsie Faye, since she's a cinch for re-election."

David continued. "Think about it, at least. We have about two weeks left and we seem to be stuck here. Channel 8 (WFAA) will be doing a story on all the races soon, and it would be good if you had something strong and memorable to say when they interview you."

I replied. "You scoff at my one on one campaigning. Many of the households I call upon have more than one voter. Neighbors talk with each other, especially the ones who are following the campaign and intend to vote. Folks talk to each other at work and at their kids' baseball and soccer games. I'll think about it while I walk this afternoon and this evening." I was walking from about 2-9:00 p.m. and was covering one or more precincts a day.

"Enid believes in her targeting and in my case with limited resources all I need is the determination to do the walks. I may not have charisma, but I have shown the determination."

Early the following week the local ABC television affiliate did a story about the race. Jim Fry, a young up and coming guy was the WFAA radio reporter covering City Hall. Since he was well versed on city issues, he was assigned to do the television story. Well, as it turns out someone else said it for me and who could have been better? To this day the only thing anyone remembers about the broadcast was Jim Fry's closing statement about the race. "And some people call Betty the North Dallas Elsie Faye Higgins."

I felt badly for Elsie Faye, being used as an example of what people in North Dallas may not like when she was just trying to speak for her constituents. But the milquetoast comment was finally answered, not by me, not by anyone in my campaign, but by the media. I felt like I had a few new friends.

ADDING GRAVITAS

Two Weeks Till Election Day

Ross Perot, the Founder of Electronic Data Systems (EDS for short) was well known in Dallas and throughout the United States, especially in finance and technology circles. In addition to his business success, he had sponsored the flying of several plane loads of Christmas dinners to the POW's in North Vietnam, led the state-wide war on drug dealers and helped shepherd the "No Pass No Play" act through the Texas Legislature. No Pass No Play meant just that. You don't participate in any extra circular activities, including sports, if your grades are not sufficient. As you would expect, many of the successful coaches in high schools in Texas were against it.

Mr. Perot had also arranged a mission by a team of EDS executives led by retired Col. Arthur D. Simmons to rescue two EDS employees, Paul Chiapparone and Bill Gaylord, from prison in Tehran at the onset of the Iranian revolution. *On Wings of Eagles* is a 1983 non-fiction thriller written by British author Ken Follett about the mission.

Mr. Perot's support would lend a lot of substance and gravitas to my campaign, whether or not he made a contribution. I had tried several avenues to reach him for a meeting. John Massey, the president of our company, tried to arrange a meeting through his friend Mort Meyerson, who was Perot's number two person at EDS. Nothing came out of every one of our attempts for a break through. My campaign seemed stalled. It needed a momentum boost that would result from a supporter like Mr. Perot.

One Monday a call came from Mr. Perot's office. He wanted to see me at 2:00 p.m. the following afternoon. *What led to the breakthrough? Was it simply that he had been traveling and was now back in town and taking an interest in the race? Was it John Massey's attempt to arrange a meeting through Mort Meyerson? Was it the Dallas Times Herald endorsement that I had recently received?*

The extent of momentum from the *Dallas Times Herald* endorsement was unknown at this point. It would depend upon the reaction to it. What caused the change was one of those questions that I've wondered about for years later but the answer really doesn't matter as much as the opportunity for a meeting.

The morning of the meeting was a fairly exciting time, thinking about how it would go, what he would say, the questions he would ask and how I would answer. I was finally going to meet this man whose career I had followed in the media and who seemed larger than life. As the morning wore on, I became anxious. By the time I reached the guard station off Forest Lane, I was afraid they would think that I looked suspicious. No problem here though. After showing proper identification, my name was quickly checked off the list and I was on my way to the main building with adrenaline rushing.

At the main building I was checked in again with the same procedure, given a visitor's badge and escorted up to Mr. Perot's office. I knew in the past that he had attempted to get the area around his headquarters' building rezoned for a reasonable increase in development rights. That attempt led to a battle royal with the neighborhoods to the west and south. North of this area contained office buildings and a large hospital lay to the east. No problem from those two directions. It was not in my district but jutted into my district from the north. That seems set up to get the zoning approved. Would he ask me about supporting the rezoning? How might I answer that question without committing to something in advance of knowing all the facts?

I was ushered into his private office, which looked like you might expect with memorabilia from his accomplishments, business and otherwise. His office was the largest one I had seen since the campaign started and he was by far the largest personality.

His first question was a softball. "So young man, come in, have a seat and tell me what you do for a living."

I knew he was very much a self-made man, not someone with a trust fund to fall back on. My reply each time the work question came up was a little different, depending upon the nature of the opinion leader and what their interest might be.

"I'm VP Corporate Planning for Gulf United Corporation, a NYSE listed investment holding company. I set up a process for our subsidiaries to develop business plans for the following year which are reviewed and approved at the corporate headquarters, after intense questioning by our CEO. Then I review the actual results each quarter and write comments for our CEO and senior management. I also work on acquisitions and have interaction with the stock analysts who follow our company. I coordinate our annual audit with our outside auditors and manage the preparation of all our SEC filings." *That was easy, so far so good.*

I spoke before he could ask another question. "Mr. Perot, I've been following your career from the beginning. I first read about you from a story in *Fortune* magazine. You grew up in Texarkana and started to work with IBM. You sold so many computers that they made you stick to a maximum quota, which you reached by mid-January and thought, what were you going to do for the rest of the year? That's when you decided to start EDS. Instead of spending a lot of cash on equipment, you simply leased unused time on a computer that you had sold to Southwestern Life Insurance Company. That was a great way to start a business without having to invest in a lot of capital. Gulf United has a lot of insurance company subsidiaries and we've consolidated data processing and other IT under a single umbrella, reminding me of what you did with EDS. That operation is like a mini EDS."

My compliments came easy because they were sincere. "I've followed the war on drugs, the Christmas dinners to the POWs, no pass no play and finally the daring rescue of your employees in Iran. I worked in Iran for two months in 1970 and then again two weeks in 1975. The first trip I was on loan to SEDCO, the international contract drilling company and the second trip was to meet with the new office for Deloitte Haskins & Sells in Tehran to discuss their participation in the audit. The last trip was close to the revolution and it was obvious that something was about to happen. The country was westernizing quickly, too quickly for some."

That seemed to convince him that I was a young man with extensive business experience and qualifications to serve on the City Council. I braced for the zoning question.

His next question was another soft ball. "What do you know about Dean Vanderbilt?"

Dean was running for the seat that represented the Lake Highlands neighborhood and Far North Dallas. His district included the one precinct that seemed to be carved out of my district and that was the one that included the EDS property.

"I've been going hell for leather since I announced and not really paid attention to the other races, except for the mayor and the two at-large seats. Before running myself, I worked in the Starke Taylor campaign. I haven't heard anything bad about Dean and since he works for Dave Fox, I assume he's a good guy." Dave Fox was a major homebuilder and civic leader.

With that he seemed to run out of questions. Mr. Perot was probably a good reader of people. He couldn't have risen as far as he had without being able to size people up quickly. Also, he probably knew not to ask me about a specific zoning case, he had more class than that. I knew it was time to "ask for the order."

"I would love to have your support and would really appreciate your giving that serious consideration."

"Thank you for coming by and good luck" was my signal that the meeting was over. I was escorted out of his office, down to the main floor and out to my car.

Boy, he was hard to read. I guess you would have to hold your cards close to the vest in all the businesses and adventures he had been in. Whether he supports me or not, I was pleased to get to meet with him privately. This was really fun! There's more to politics than just winning an election.

That was Monday and on Wednesday a check for $500 from Mr. Perot hit our little campaign office. A few days later the contribution reports were filed, and both newspapers picked up on the contribution, which was tantamount to an endorsement. Whew, I got the *Times Herald* and Ross Perot. Momentum is building and I was feeling sky high. The meeting with Ross Perot, someone whose business career I had idolized along with his support meant a lot to me.

The next person on my list to meet was another Dallas icon, former mayor and co-founder, chairman and CEO of Texas Instruments, Inc., Eric Jonsson. Mayor Jonsson was a strong advocate for education, having served on or led the boards of many educational institutions and created alliances to improve local educational facilities. Jonsson was a founder of the Southwest Center for Advanced Studies, which later became the University of Texas at Dallas and where I went to graduate school and now work as a part time lecturer.

In 1964, shortly after the assassination of President John F. Kennedy, Jonsson became mayor of Dallas. He worked to improve morale and the image of the city. He was reelected three times. Jonsson pushed through a $175 million bond program that financed a new city hall building, the Dallas Convention Center and the Dallas Central Library. Dallas is not a sea port or a river port, only a city on the prairie with no reason for being other than the optimism and drive of its leaders. Mayor Jonsson was a central leader in the development of Dallas/Fort Worth International Airport, which is now Dallas' port to the outside world. By 1983, a Gallop poll of the United States found that the Dallas Cowboys had surpassed the Kennedy assassination as the number one association about the city in the country's collective mind.

His office called my campaign and asked for a visit. "Another one of my hero's and now I get to meet him in person," I told Ruth. "Mayor Jonsson is someone I would love to get to meet whether he supported me or not."

When the day came, I went to his office, one of those downtown Dallas offices of a prominent retired person with absolutely nothing to prove. Well appointed, but not ostentatious. An original painting or two and authentic Persian rugs on hardwood floors. He had the usual administrative assistant-gate-keeper in the outer office.

I feel like a kid coming to see one of my hero's. Please, Jim, try to act like an adult even though you are in the presence of one of the most respected leaders in Texas.

"Hello, I'm Jim Richards and I have a two o'clock appointment with Mayor Jonsson." I nervously said to the gatekeeper." I'm a little early because I wasn't sure how long it would take me to get here."

"Go on in, he's expecting you."

As I entered his office I felt surrounded by the aura of a great person, who was all about doing what's best for the City and our Country. "Mayor Jonsson, hello. I'm Jim Richards and I'm a candidate for the Dallas City Council, District 3."

"Yes, of course you are. Sit down and tell me what you're all about."

With that he walked out from behind his desk and took a seat next to me. What a class guy!

"I'm a businessman, a vice president with Gulf United Corporation and I spent ten years with Deliotte Haskins & Sells, the CPA firm before that. I've served on the Dallas Civil Service Board, and the board of the Dallas County Community Action Agency, the agency that administers all the war on poverty programs in Dallas County. I worked as a volunteer on the last city bond election and presently serve on two halfway house boards. I've chaired the finance and the ushering and greeting committees of my church, Preston Hollow United Methodist Church. I'm married and have a two-year-old son. One of my first civic endeavors was to serve as a discussion leader in your latest, Goals for Dallas Program. And finally, I went to graduate school at a University you co-founded, UT Dallas. I have an MA degree in Political Economy, with a concentration in Urban/Regional."

His interest perked up at the last statement, having been instrumental in the founding of UT Dallas. He nodded and smiled.

"Okay, why are you running? Why do you want to be on the City Council?

"Mayor Jonsson, I'm from a small town in East Texas called Grapeland. I got an early lesson in civic action from my father and his fellow citizen boosters. He and his friends didn't want to see Grapeland dry up and become a ghost town like so many small towns in Texas and throughout the Midwest. The town doctor was retiring. These guys worked and worked and raised money and finally built a community hospital and recruited a dynamic young doctor to move to Grapeland and set up a practice."

"That's always a good move. Health care should be a priority," interjected the former mayor.

I nodded and continued. "The area was dependent upon agriculture and oil field services so there were no new jobs to keep the kids from moving away after high school. They set about on an economic development quest to bring a manufacturing plant to town. After learning that the water supply was inadequate, they worked to have a county lake built close to town and then recruited Nucor Corporation to build a steel joist plant, which is still there, by the way."

"Another good move, "the former mayor again interjected.

"And while I love being from a small town, I'm enjoying this dynamic City. I appreciate all the amenities and opportunities because I grew up without them. I want to contribute and help, like my father did, especially with transportation and other traffic issues."

"I see. Well one of the first things that you need to put in the next bond election is a computerized traffic signal system which will automatically adjust to inclement weather and the flow of traffic. Those systems are amazing."

"I will remember that after I'm elected. Mr. Mayor, I thank you for the meeting and the information and would really appreciate your support in the election."

"Good luck to you in the election. Your opponent and my wife have had a few tiffs."

With that, I knew what had just happened. I understand what the meeting was about. That was an interview to make sure I was an okay guy before he supported me.

The next week a $500 contribution and a pledge card from former Mayor Jonsson showed up at my headquarters. Everybody in the campaign was in awe when they saw it.

That same evening, I returned home from an afternoon and evening of precinct walks to the sound of the phone ringing. It was Jerry Bartos, a board member of the North Dallas Chamber of Commerce. He was well known throughout the city and most folks assumed he would run for City Council once Joe Haggar retired. But like many others, he was intimidated by Ebby's support for Betty and they shared the same support base among the real estate community. He, like most of his Chamber colleagues, had endorsed Betty so why would he be calling me?

"Jim, this is Jerry Bartos. How are you doing tonight?"

"Why Jerry, I'm just fine, and how about you and how is your family?

By this time I was hyper-vigilant to tricksters.

"I'm well, Jim. Business is good, my health is good, and my family is as well. Thanks for asking."

"How can I help you?"

His answer. "Well Jim, I'm calling on behalf of the board of the North Dallas Chamber of Commerce. As you know, many of us have endorsed Betty because of her civic work in North Dallas and Ebby's support as well. We couldn't really refuse a request of Ebby Halliday; she's done so much for the City and Chamber."

My curiosity peaked. Even though I was tired from a day campaigning, I stood swaying from one foot to the other.

Jerry droned on. "We at the NDCC recognize that this is turning into a real competitive race and we wanted you to know that however it turns out, we would like to be friends."

"Jerry, I'd want to be your friend anyway, you're a good guy, no matter what Tom James says about you or about me. You've done the Dallas area and Dallas Independent School District a great service already."

I could hear a sigh of relief. "Okay, Jim, thanks for your kind comments and good luck to you the rest of the way. Let's get together after the election when you have time."

"Jerry, thanks for calling."

I hesitated for a moment then told myself, why not? "By the way, it would be rude if I didn't take this opportunity to ask for your support and your vote. Can I count on you?"

Jerry seemed a little taken aback but replied. "Well gee, Jim, you are a good candidate. Goodbye, now."

The day was Saturday. I went into our little campaign office beaming. Buck was already there talking to Ruth.

"Of all people Jerry Bartos called me last night, representing the NDCC board and saying he thought it had developed into a real competitive race and that they wanted to be friends after the election win or lose. Do you believe that?"

Buck said, "Of course they do. Usually organizations like that, who get involved in government, may like to have members supporting both sides so they are covered no matter who wins. They have a big bet down on Betty and are realizing they need to hedge. Maybe Ebby pushed them all too hard, maybe they thought Betty's election was a foregone conclusion but for whatever reason, now they have decided they need to hedge their bet. It's a really good sign for us."

I was in a celebratory mood. "Let's celebrate tonight after the day's campaigning is over. Let's go to Joe's. It might be good to be seen there celebrating. I'll call Lisa and ask her if she wants to join us."

Buck and I adored Lisa. She made phone calls for three hours at campaign headquarters almost every evening.

I called her later that day. "Lisa, Buck and I are meeting at Joe's after the day's campaigning is over for a little celebration of sorts. We both hope you will join us for a drink. Can you come by at about 9:00?" She agreed, and the party was on.

I got to Joe's right after my precinct walks for the afternoon and evening. Buck and Lisa were already there sitting at one of the few tables. Lisa asked, "So what are we celebrating?"

Buck had stopped by the Dallas Morning News late that Saturday afternoon for an early edition of the Sunday paper. His answer was new news for me as well as Lisa. "We now have both newspaper endorsements."

"Great, you must have obtained an advance copy of the Sunday edition," I said.

"Yes, if you hang around there late on a Saturday afternoon you can score an early version of the Sunday paper.

"I really couldn't get a feel for the *Dallas Time Herald*. I'd been interviewed by Ron Calhoun, the major political reporter who covered partisan politics. I was cautiously optimistic about the *Dallas Morning News*. Hank Tatum, who was on the editorial board and Op Ed pages, conducted the interview. His questions were more municipal related than partisan."

Shirley Miller, a buddy of mine from the 1980 George H.W. Bush campaign, lived two houses down from where Jetta and I lived. Shirley's husband was on the editorial staff. She kept saying, "You're getting the endorsement."

"But what about all the ads that the real estate folks place in the *Morning News*? Not just Ebby but all of them."

"The editorial board doesn't consider that. The realtors need the paper as much as the paper needs the realtors. And not all realtors support Betty. Many of them feel like they are competing with Ebby."

Buck put things in perspective. "Anyway, we've survived their verbal assaults and have a good footing for the final two weeks. Let's lick our wounds and celebrate our good fortune."

I added. "There's more. Jerry Bartos called me last night, representing the NDCC board and saying he thought it had developed into a real competitive race and that they wanted to be friends after the election win or lose."

"That's great. Are you beginning to relax a little now?" Lisa asked.

"In a campaign that lasts only two months there hasn't been any time to relax. It's been up against the wall the whole time. You can't make any time up since the time involved is finite. That's what we are doing tonight. I realize it's after 9:00 p.m. but we are relaxing and celebrating."

I felt like we were really getting close to winning, barring a catastrophe. Both money and endorsements were coming in. For the first time, it seemed like the election might be ours to lose.

FREE THE RICHARDS' THREE

One and a Half Weeks Till Election Day

I was an optimistic young man with high hopes of being elected. The campaign was not wearing me down, even though it was two months of seven days a week of neighborhood walks, rain or shine. There was no time to waste on being tired for every moment was valuable. During the first month, there was a little time to clean up mistakes. Now time was running out. I wanted to meet as many voters as I could, and there was only about 10 days left. I had no premonition that a catastrophe was close by.

About 10:30 p.m. one fateful night four of my volunteers called with a scheme up their sleeves.

"We're tired of seeing Betty's yard signs illegally placed in the Preston Road right of way and plan to lift a few of them."

"Where are we meeting?"

"Not we, Jim, you're not going. Are you crazy? What if we get caught?"

"Maybe so," I admitted. I must have been half asleep.

As luck would have it, or not, they were caught. A Dallas police officer spotted them in the act and made a gallant arrest of three of the four. The driver, Bill Booher, was not arrested, even though he was abetting the crime.

I was tipped off about the arrest later that night by Dan Garrigan, a good friend and a top-notch defense attorney. The three who were arrested had engaged Dan to obtain their release from jail with his bail account.

Dan was laughing as he said it. "Three of your campaign workers have been arrested and taken to jail. They were lifting one of Betty's yard signs in the Preston Road right of way at a church at Preston and Churchill Way. I'm on my way to bail those bad guys out of jail before a really bad guy does them in."

"Okay, thanks for doing this Dan. "I laughed at first but didn't instantly understand the potential of the situation. However, as I thought about how close I came to going to jail one night as a teenager, the gravity of the situation set in.

It was a hot summer night. After about an hour of drag racing, the participants, including me, and the spectators backed our cars into the curb on Main Street in Grapeland, my small home town. We immediately heard sirens screaming and three sheriff cruisers pulled up, blocking us so no one could leave.

A huge man jumped out of the first cruiser, ran over to us and yelled, "All right, who's been drag racing out there on that egg and butter road?" The road was nicknamed that because of the chicken and dairy farms in that part of the county. The man was Houston County Sheriff J.B. Lively. J.B. was one of those southern sheriffs we used to see in the news reels about the civil rights marches. Bull Conner, the Selma, Alabama, Sherriff, who turned his dogs and nightstick wielding deputies on the marchers, had nothing on J.B. Lively. No one said a word. We just stood there, frozen in our tracks and afraid to speak. J.B. was probably 6'4" but at the time he seemed ten feet tall. Finally, Johnny Bird, who hadn't been racing at all but whose car had a flat tire, started trying to change the tire of his family sedan.

J.B. looked at Johnny and yelled. "Somebody better say something or you're all going to jail."

Innocent sounding Johnny answered him. "I'm just trying to change a flat tire."

J.B. turned to his deputies. "Take him in first." Two deputies handcuffed and manhandled poor Johnny into the back of one of their cruisers.

He's really serious. Some of us, hell all of us are in big trouble now. What are we going to do?

Then the Sherriff turned to the rest of us. I could tell he recognized me. "If I don't get confessions quick, we're going to take you guys out on that grass and show you what the rough side of a peanut paddy is like."

Now that was a juvenile remark for a grown man to say but it's scary as hell.

J.B. was from the Grapeland side of Houston County and had a sprawling ranch outside of town. He had run my father's gas station for a while before running for sheriff, so I knew him from earlier in life. Since he was elected sheriff, his wealth had grown considerably, compared to what a small county pays their sheriff. Hell, even the county commissioners had day jobs. I remembered delivering a load of gasoline to J.B.'s ranch on behalf of my father, a wholesale gasoline dealer. As I was pumping the gas into a skid tank I watched convicts who were serving time in the county jail working on his ranch. They were baling hay, a hard, hot dirty job. He was there and knew that I had seen them. He knew that I knew what he was doing. Hoping to take advantage of that and taking a calculated risk, I announced "Sheriff Lively, how about we just all go home and forget about doing this again ever."

He stood there with legs planted and arms folded, staring at me for what seemed to be about an hour, and then finally spoke. "Okay, get outta here now and don't ever let me catch you doing this again." The big sheriff and his posse of deputies then went back to the county seat in Crockett, with Johnny Bird, the token arrest for the night. Johnny was released the next day without being charged.

I headed home. My drag racing days were over. It was time to find a tamer form of excitement. Looking back on it, that incident could have been my first time to think politically.

Typically, this yard sign incident wouldn't have amounted to much of a news story except for the people involved. There were a couple of big names among the group, David Johnson and Tony Garrett. Tony was not only the media consultant for Jerry Rucker but was also a special assistant to the Speaker of the Texas House of Representatives. The third member of the group was Buck Wynne. Buck wasn't famous yet but would eventually become chairman of the Texas Water Commission and then ran the federal EPA's Regional office in Dallas. Unfortunately, the next day was a slow news day and by mid-morning both papers were working on the story. Both planned big spreads about the incident. Enid had been tipped off through her extensive network and told me to call Betty right away and apologize. A feeling of dread crept over me as I made the call from home before going to headquarters.

When she answered, I was brief. "Betty, it's Jim Richards. I'm sorry that some of my overzealous campaign workers pulled up your yard signs." I stopped short of claiming no knowledge of the prank beforehand.

"Okay, thanks for calling" was all she said before she hung up the phone.

She's laughing, I know she is. She believes the campaign is over and she has won. She very well could be right.

Reporters from both newspapers called for a statement. I could tell they were enjoying the moment; this sort of thing doesn't happen every day and they knew all the participants. It was an interesting news story for them while covering a rather uneventful race for mayor and they likely were laughing under their breath.

The reporters were on deadline, so the questions came quickly and to the point. "Okay, Jim. Do you have anything to say about the yard sign caper? Three of your volunteers went to jail last night. That's JAIL!"

Maybe a little humor will disarm them. "Oh, were they my volunteers?" Everyone laughed.

"Seriously, it was just some overzealous campaign volunteers who saw that the signs were illegally placed in the right of way and decided to take action themselves rather than wait for the city to clean them up. I've already called Betty and apologized." That was my official statement to the reporters. *Please, just print the official one.*

They're no longer laughing with me. They're laughing at me now. I know they

One of David Crosby's songs includes the phrase *"Paranoia is looking in your rear view mirror and seeing a Po lees car."* Well the police car was on the scene about 12 hours ago and paranoia was rushing in now. I couldn't get the incident out of my mind. It's all I could think about. *Everyone is laughing at me and the campaign. What the hell am I going to do? What can I do to make up for this? The campaign was progressing nicely and now this. It was worse than the milquetoast comment.*

The phone rang. Ruth was on the line. "Jim, I'm sorry about what happened last night and the fact that everyone in town seems to know about it."

"Yes, Ruth, I'm sure everyone knows about it, thanks to radio and two daily newspapers."

Ruth had more bad news. "By the way, Betty's campaign has scheduled a champagne celebration for tonight. They believe they've won and aren't waiting until election day to celebrate. They'll have a regular victory party then."

"Victory party, huh. Gee, you're full of good news, aren't you?"

"Yep, but hang on for there is more to the story. C.P. Henry, a campaign manager and consultant had tee shirts printed with "Free the Richards 3" across the front and they're selling like hotcakes. The tee shirts are blue with white lettering." The slogan was reminiscent of the Chicago 7 (or 8) arrested during the 1968 Democratic National Convention in Chicago and the efforts to obtain their release, including the slogan "Free the Chicago 7." The media loved stuff like this. This was the only race with any kind of excitement.

Ruth's advice, "Keep going. Hit the streets and start knocking on doors. The exercise will make you feel better and the voters you contact will appreciate you showing up after the incident and giving them a chance to scold or raze you."

"I'm on my way now to the precinct east of Hillcrest and south of Park Lane, anchored by Temple Emanuel. That's one of the few precincts I haven't covered yet."

It was a cool, clear sunny day in late-February. Many people were outside, enjoying the pleasant weather happy that the winter was fizzling out. Folks were puttering around in their yards, visiting with their neighbors and supervising children playing outside. I approached everyone that was outside and introduced myself. Many razzed me about the yard sign incident but thought it was funny.

I walked, knocked on doors and shook hands for the rest of the afternoon and evening until my mandatory cut off at 9:00 p.m. I needed to unwind so I drove around in my car for about a half hour, then true to my routine, picked up a hamburger at Jack-in- the Box and headed home. The house was dark except for a single light in the kitchen. Jetta and Murk were both asleep. I sat alone, savored the hamburger and felt the stress of the day slide away with each swallow of my favorite kind of beer, a COLD beer. The precinct walk and the interaction with people during the walk had taken most of the sting out of the incident. Betty's campaign may be celebrating but the folks I'd met that afternoon seemed amused by the yard sign debacle.

One thing I hadn't thought about before entering the race was being a target for people bearing a grudge. Jetta had received a speeding ticket right before I entered the race and with the help of Dan Garrigan, she went to court and got the ticket dismissed. A day or so after the yard sign incident, a police officer came to our door and served Jetta with a notice that he had refiled the ticket and that she would have to go to court again. Dan told us later that the same officer who wrote the ticket in the first place and then refiled it was the officer who made the arrest of the Richards Three. Coincidence? I don't think so. I was going to have to get used to things like this and no, whether I'm elected or not, I won't make a complaint to the city manager or tell anyone else.

For anyone contemplating a political race, you need to be prepared for things like this. Don't let it discourage you from running, just understand and accept that this could happen. You deal with it and go on about your business of either running or serving.

My redemption came rather quickly. The next morning I was at headquarters picking up my daily walk list and returning phone calls. The night callers on the phones at headquarters left me a list of folks wanting to talk to the candidate. After making most call backs, a call came in from Enid.

"You know those full page ads that Starke Taylor's mayoral campaign has been running in the two newspapers showing off his endorsements."

"Sure, I've seen them. They run in the Metro section. Usually on the back page," I replied.

"The Taylor campaign is getting a lot of comments about them. They're getting a lot of attention. Everybody has started looking for the ads to see what names are in them. That's the reason for my call. No other candidate except Taylor is doing it and if you run one on a day he doesn't, folks will look for his and see yours. It will put the perception of you and your campaign on almost the same level as Taylor. We need something positive after our boys got arrested the other night."

"How much would one of those ads cost?" My stomach knotted up because I was worried we had spent everything that had come in. We were broke at a time when we needed to do something to offset the fallout from the yard sign caper.

"I can get it done turnkey for about $8,500 (over $20,000 in 2020 dollars). I just got off the phone with Booher. We have zero cash in the bank. If you win, of course you can raise that much easily. If you lose, that will have to be paid for out of your personal funds. They'll run the ad on credit based on your personal guarantee. What do you want to do?"

This was the kind of decision that makes or breaks a campaign. If I didn't win it could take years to pay off the debt. My day job was in jeopardy, not only because I'd chosen to campaign and was going to work part time if I won, but our CEO had decided this was a great time to sell. Our business sectors were at the peak of their price cycles. I was scared.

As usual, Enid has a great strategy. Am I in this or not? Am I willing to make a total commitment to win? How much am I willing to sacrifice to this effort for fifty dollars a week? Boy, this is a gut-wrenching decision. I've got too much invested in time and reputation not to go all out and do whatever I need to do to solidify my efforts.

My decisions to say no to something take a long time and a lot more stewing. The ones to say yes, not so long. It took all of ten seconds to make this one.

"Let's go with it. Let's do it. We're going to win, come hell or high water. Buy the ad. I will personally guarantee payment."

Oftentimes winning requires total commitment, whether in politics, business or sports. Commitment and determination can trump a shortage of money, intelligence or charisma. I was all in now and rushed out of headquarters with my list of houses to call on that day. The feedback from the citizens I met that day was encouraging.

The next morning I grabbed the Metro Section of the *Dallas Morning News* where the ad had run. It looked great. The Taylor campaign hadn't run an ad that day. It must have been a coincidence at least that was the position Enid would take. The page included the endorsements of the *Dallas Morning News*, the *Dallas Times Herald* and the Police and Fire Fighters Association. It also included all my supporter's names, Democrats, Republicans and Independents, including four former Council members and two former mayors. I was proud of the ad and didn't worry about the cost. I felt good about doing it now, seeing the ad and how closely it resembled the Taylor campaign ad. That decision had been made and there was no looking back. I had warned Jetta about the cost and she took it in stride.

As usual, I walked again. Time was running out.

That evening, the NBC affiliate in our sister city Fort Worth, ran a spoof story about the yard sign incident. They gave a brief analysis of the race and called the district the "Silk Stocking District". The reporter was friends with David and Tony and was amused and made fun of the whole incident. The story ended with a call from the police to Betty's campaign treasurer to ask if they wanted to press charges.

According to the television spoof "Book 'Em, Danno" was said to be his reply, right out of the Hawaii Five O TV series.

The stakes are higher than ever. Not only my reputation and emotional wellbeing are on the line but my personal funds (that I will have to make, somehow) are too. We have to win this thing!

Other than last minute electioneering, the campaign was virtually over, win or lose. Time had almost run out. It was becoming too late to correct any mistakes.

Bill Booher had been urging me for several days to write a concession speech. "If you lose you will first need to call Betty and concede, then tell your supporters who show up at the victory party. You won't be in any shape or mood to come up with a concession speech then."

I wasn't going there. "Bill, I don't want to spend any of the precious time that is left doing anything but campaigning." The real reason was that I just wasn't ready to consider a defeat and the downer that would follow.

Time was running out. I was exhausted but didn't know it. I went over and over the entire campaign in my head. For the last two months I rarely had time to think, much less reflect on the whole campaign, using every available hour to try to meet more voters. I had faced the prospect of running but didn't have the courage until Enid Gray, through Steve Bartlett, encouraged me to do so.

At first, I wasn't going to give up my exciting job to run when faced with our company's CEO's initial refusal. I toiled away in the Taylor for Mayor Campaign until Enid (I suspected) convinced Starke to send a delegation to convince Mr. Fitts to let me run.

I was able to obtain endorsements from every group I sought except those related to real estate. I had expected the Police and Fire Association to go with Betty because they knew her from the Crime Watch Program. As it turned out, they went with me. Both newspapers endorsed me.

I learned many lessons about local elections. As is the case in many elections, the down ballot candidates get much less media publicity than those at the top of the ticket. The news media tend to cover the impolite over the political, even in local elections. People tend to vote for candidates who respond to their ideas with dignity and respect and spend less time talking and more time listening. Folks would rather vote for candidates they have met or who have made an attempt to meet them. Meeting a candidate face to face, especially unexpectedly, creates a moment to be remembered.

The focus of our campaign was to meet as many people as possible, to make it personal. We were lucky to have the controversies that captured the attention of the media, giving our side a lot of favorable air time and print space. The cost of the full page ad, the printing and mailing of brochures didn't compare to the value of all the free media we got because the race was controversial in a time when none of the others were.

Finally, most local elections for mayors, City Council and school board members are non-partisan, meaning you don't run or serve as a Democrat or Republican. In today's highly partisan climate of treating members of the other party as the enemy, running and serving in a non-partisan way helps both sides see members of the other party not as enemies but as colleagues and allies who can work together and get things done.

TIME HAS EXPIRED

Election Day Eve and Election Day

The last day of the campaign was over. The election was the next day. As I drove home, I saw that the lights were on at Tony Garret's home, so I decided to drop by.

"Jim Richards, come in and have a cold beer," was his warm greeting.

We sat down in Tony's living room in the front of the house to talk.

"How's one of the infamous Richards 3 faring? How is your candidate Mr. Rucker faring?"

"Tony Garrett is fine. The Rucker race is very close and will most likely end up in a run off. Let's talk about your race. Are you prepared to accept the outcome if you lose?"

"I haven't considered it. I've spent all my time campaigning and yeah, I know, time for that has run out except to work in front of the polls tomorrow."

Tony agreed." You should. You've made a valiant attempt with your two-month campaign but you entered the race late. It wasn't any fault of yours and Betty had a head start of seven months."

"So, she started in June and I started in January. What did she do between July and January? When Ebby got her all that backing in the first month all she did was show up at a few meetings." *Am I whistling past the graveyard? Maybe I should listen to Tony and Booher, they are both pros and I'm just an amateur.*

"On the other hand, you're right. I should spend tonight facing up to a possible defeat and working on a concession speech."

"I'm sorry, Jim. Go home and get some rest. You've got twelve hours of working polling sites ahead of you tomorrow. Vote yourself, then hit the high turnout precincts and make a last attempt to meet people. When people come to vote in the mayor's race, they will meet you just before they cast their vote."

"Thanks for the beer and the advice."

As I walked in the front door it was late, Murk was in bed so the house was quiet.

Jetta greeted me. "There's leftovers in the refrigerator."

After I ate, Jetta came into the kitchen and sat down across the table from me. I could tell she wanted to talk. "You might want to think about how to handle it if you lose. I hope that doesn't happen but some of your friends today may abandon you after tomorrow."

"I hate to think about it that way."

"I want you to be realistic, if you accept the possibility of losing now it will be easier tomorrow if the results go against you."

What is up? Three people in a row have warned me about losing. Am I missing something?

"Jetta, you're the third person in a row who has warned me about losing in the last 12 hours. Three warnings in a row. How many witches encouraged Macbeth to murder the king? Three!"

Jetta replied. "They didn't warn him of the risk of doing it, they encouraged him to do it; just the opposite of the warnings you've received." With that, she turned around and went to bed.

I tossed and turned that night, thinking about worse-case scenarios. I continued to worry but also continued to reflect on the campaign. It had changed me in several ways. Even though I'm an introvert, I got over that quickly. While not completely fearless, I was much less so than when this endeavor began and wiser as well. *This time tomorrow I'll know, win or lose.* I felt like a different person than I was nine months ago.

I woke early the next morning, without an alarm clock. It was election day, first Saturday in March, 1983. I spent the day going from precinct to precinct, one last time, pitching myself to voters as they came to vote. Most came to vote in the larger race for mayor of Dallas.

The contact with voters lifted my spirit. I felt well received. People smiled when we shook hands. I'll always remember the quote from President Lyndon Johnson. *"If you can't work a room and in 15 minutes know who is for you and who is against you, you don't belong in politics."*

As Tony Garrett recommended, I voted at my home precinct then went to the western part of the district with the intention of working my way back to the middle by the time the polls closed. About 10:30 that morning I hit Betty's precinct and worked it for at least an hour until, low and behold, she shows up. Her husband followed behind her up the sidewalk, walking slowly, shoulders slouched.

I was nervous about the unavoidable exchange.

"Good Morning Betty. It's good to see you. I hope you're doing well." With that I extended my hand for a handshake.

Betty glared at me for a few seconds then finally spoke. "Hello Jim". It sounded like Jerry Seinfeld when he sees his nemesis Newman. "Hello Newman."

"You've got a lot of nerve coming over here in my precinct, my Crime Watch area. My Crime Watch captains have been calling me, telling me where you were and what you were doing."

At least while I was campaigning today you were at home to take all those calls from your crime watch captains.

As they strode by I tried to speak to her husband, hoping to finally meet him. "Hi". I made a friendly attempt and extended my hand and gave him as sympathetic a look as I could muster. He shook my hand, looking down, avoiding eye contact. Betty grabbed his other hand and pulled him toward the elementary school that served as a polling place.

After that unpleasant encounter I started heading east and spent the rest of the day doing more of the same. As far as I could tell, Lee Rittenberry, the Tea Party candidate who also entered the race late and I were the only ones working the polls that day in this district. The Tea Party of the 1980's wasn't nearly the Tea Party of today. Then it consisted of a few older retired men who seemed to take pleasure in being against everything, especially bond elections. That described Lee to a tea, or tee.

Lee and I moved more or less together for the rest of the day. He had started in the west, as I had and was working his way east. Lee's budget for the race was whatever he spent on gasoline. His campaigning, other than today, was to attend events and forums and present his case there. I showed respect for Lee and he appreciated it. He probably thought Betty was going to win and viewed me as more of a traveling buddy with the same objectives than as an opponent.

As the day wore on, more and more folks came out to vote. The election had a high turnout, especially for a non-partisan municipal government race. Lee and I went precinct to precinct together, all in the western part of the district.

The positive reception I received from most of the voters added to my confidence. Most folks appeared glad to see me and to meet a candidate on the ballot where they were about to vote. A few of the voters kidded me about "The Richards 3".

My response was "I'm sure they thought they were doing a service for the community," which usually got a good laugh.

I finished the day at a swing precinct at W.T. White High School close to Midway Road, in about the center of Northwest Dallas. Betty's strength lay mostly west of Midway and mine mostly east of Midway, where I lived, worked in my church and where two important Jewish Temples were located.

The polls had just closed and it was freezing outside so Lee and I went in to the polling place to warm ourselves.

The voting for the precinct at W.T. White High School was in the lobby of the high school building. The election judge was opening the voting machine as I was walking in. The machine had a meter which showed the vote totals for each race so one could glance in and see who won that precinct's contribution to the entire district or the entire City.

"Hi, I'm Jim Richards. May I see the results?"

"I know who you are." She was one of Betty's supporters. After seeing the vote herself, she warmed up a little and waved me over to take a look.

"You did okay and that this might be a competitive race after all. If you need help with anything after the election, let me know."

"I will and thank you." I peered inside to see that I had won this precinct in the geographic and political middle of the voting district. My vote total exceeded both of Betty's and Lee's so that was a good sign. I headed home.

The race was over. The polls had closed and there was no more voting, no more electioneering. It was a great feeling. I breathed a sigh of relief, knowing that there was nothing left to do and I had done my best. Win or lose, it was over. I relaxed for the first time since that January evening when I got word that the campaign was probably back on. I drove home slowly, enjoying a respite from the frantic last two months. Based on what I perceived to be a swing precinct, I had probably won.

Finally, I pulled into the driveway. Jetta met me at the door. "Lisa Saeman called. She's at your campaign office tallying up the votes. She arranged for someone at the court house to call her and keep her updated as election judges bring in their results. It looks really bad for you. Betty is winning but I haven't told your mother so don't say anything." My mother had come up from East Texas for the election and to spend time with Murk.

Based on what I had just observed, I wasn't as worried as Jetta. "Maybe the precincts in Betty's end of the district finished tabulating their vote first. I just left a swing precinct in the middle of the district and I had won that precinct without a runoff."

Jetta wasn't showing much emotion. She was all business. "Well, your mother and Murk and I are heading to the party."

"Go ahead. I'll see you there in about thirty minutes. I need to settle down and get cleaned up after twelve hours of electioneering."

Time to clean up and prepare for the party, victory or not.

I took a quick shower, imaging two scenarios; first one losing then second one winning. While getting ready I focused on what I had to be thankful for: my family and friends, my health and the job I still had. Finally ready, I got in my car and headed for the headquarters.

After Jetta's news about Betty being ahead in the early reporting precincts, I wondered if I was being delusional about winning. I wondered if anyone running for office might be a little delusional. The same might apply to inventors, artists and others who attempt to alter the status quo. Perhaps folks being a little delusional is how progress gets made.

For the past week, our campaign manager kept insisting "We have to plan for a victory party."

My answer all last week was. "I don't want to waste time on that, the election isn't over. We can put a little something together if we win. What makes you so sure there will be one?" I was grasping for any assurances that would assuage my doubts.

Ruth pointed to a copy of the newspaper ad that we had pinned on a wall in the campaign office. Look at these endorsements. Unless they catch you in a compromising position, we're going to win."

"Ruth, I hope you're right but you and Booher will have to be in charge of any party. Bill has been hounding me for a week to draft a concession speech, in case we lose. I haven't taken the time for that either."

It was about 8:30 p.m. when I reached the campaign office, which was already packed with people. Lisa was waiting for me at the door.

"Things look much better now. The early results were mainly from Betty's end of town and now the Inwood, Preston and Hillcrest precincts are reporting and you could win without a runoff."

I breathed a sigh of relief. "Whew, I kinda thought so, based on the precinct where I closed the day. It's in the middle of the district and that precinct had us winning without a runoff. Let's hope we can keep it up."

As the voting results continued to trickle in, I walked around the room greeting everyone and visiting with anybody that came by to wish me well. I thanked everybody for their help. Many of the well-wishers hadn't been involved in the campaign but I didn't care. The more the merrier. Winners need to consolidate their position. I believed I had won and couldn't hide my excitement no matter how hard I tried. I looked around the room for Jetta and my mother but couldn't find them.

"Any word from Betty yet?" I asked nobody in particular. Lisa answered, "Not yet. Someone from their campaign called earlier to make sure they had the right location and phone number. We got theirs and gave them ours."

David Johnson stormed in about 10:30. "We're going downtown! The mayor and the at-large candidates are having victory parties at Union Station and all the media are there. I'll arrange for you to give them some quotes. Come with me and I'll drive us down there." Since the party at my office was dying down, I said goodbye to my family and told them where we were going. Booher and I got in David's car and we were off to Union Station.

There was a note to call Lisa when we arrived at Union Station. "Betty called to concede right after you left. You don't need to call her back. She said she was going home."

Betty and I must have split the Republican votes and I had to have won the Democrat votes, allowing me to win without a run-off. How do I know that? Exit polls? No. We couldn't afford any polls and the newspapers didn't care. You know from intuition and looking at who is on support lists and who made the political contributions to each campaign.

It was official. I had won the election! While the time leading up to the campaign when I didn't have permission to run seemed to drag on forever, the two months of the actual campaign flew by. I was in a trance, a dream world, walking around Union Station with David.

I wanted to be surrounded by my family and friends and the people who helped me overcome the hurdles that made this moment possible. I'd never experienced the kind of euphoria I felt that night and savored every moment of achieving a dream. I've heard the expression, time stood still. When you feel like I did that night, time doesn't even seem to exist.

The campaign was over and the pressure was off. David was reveling in his role of media consultant. He always seemed to be in a good mood, laughing about everything. I gave both newspapers and KRLD Radio quotes I had used throughout the campaign. I couldn't stop laughing and hugging everyone I came in contact with. I had won and was going to do a good job.

After David drove Bill and I back to our headquarters, the party continued for a while. Jetta, my mother and Murk went home fairly early and almost everyone else was gone by midnight. Bill Booher asked me to go with him to his house to pick up their baby sitter and take her home. On the drive we talked about the campaign and what I planned to do. I wanted to carry the momentum of the campaign into the office and represent well the citizens of my district. I finally got home about 2:00 a.m. and totally exhausted, fell right to sleep.

At 6:00 a.m. the phone rang. "Jim, its Steve Bartlett. Congratulations on your victory. I wasn't able to reach you last night and wanted to talk before you got away."

"Thank you, Steve. Thank you for all your help. I hope my using your name doesn't get you in too much trouble with Ebby."

"Whatever. We'll work through whatever happens. Good luck and enjoy the time between winning the election and the inauguration. Then the real work begins. You've won a victory for the neighborhoods all over the City and you need to use that victory to shield them from unplanned and uncontrolled over development."

"I fully intend to. Thanks again for all your help, goodbye."

For as long as I could remember, I had a duty to whatever job I happen to have at the time. Later, duty to my family emerged. Now, in addition to job and family, I had a duty to the folks in my district and to the City as a whole. This responsibility was certainly larger than myself, which is what I had been looking for all along. It felt great!

Maybe I was a little overly optimistic about someday moving forward to higher levels of service, but that night, I didn't care. Working on the local level was going to be fun. Here, with non-partisan elections, unlike national level, Democrats and Republicans worked together. There's no Republican or Democratic way to fill potholes, build streets and pick up garbage. The federal government can be mired in partisan gridlock and debt but here at the local level we must have a balanced budget and must work together.

I learned a lot in this campaign and highly recommend anyone, especially young people, with an interest in government to get involved. A campaign itself, is many people, not just the candidate, who is more like a vessel for the campaign. Working on something larger than oneself is an exciting and satisfying accomplishment. It's like being on a team and working with your teammates. If you can make it a cause, that's more important than the candidate, you are better off.

My message to anyone interested in politics is:

Never sell determination short. It can beat ideology, age, experience, gender, intelligence, money, and even charisma. Make friends with like-minded people. By like-minded, I mean folks who want to be involved and want to be helpful. People in general are good and want to do the right thing. Volunteer for a campaign, not just a candidate election but bond elections as well. Make friends with other volunteers and the candidates. Volunteer to serve on a city or county board or commission. You'll learn more about how government works from the inside and how to influence it. The experience will build your self-confidence and develop leadership skills. It takes a good leader to lead volunteers who work without getting paid. Additional civic opportunities may come your way, which will lead to making more friends.

If you like the experience, RUN YOURSELF.

EPILOGUE

The months of March and April of 1983 were heady times for some but stressful for others. The first round of elections was over and those of us who won without a runoff were able to bask in the spotlight, relax and enjoy that period before the real work began. The two African-American members, Elsie Faye Higgins and Fred Blair, representing South Dallas and South Oak Cliff, respectively, won handily. Jim Hart, a dentist representing north Oak Cliff and the venerable Max Goldblatt, representing Southeast Dallas were also winners without a runoff.

Starke Taylor was to be mayor and my new friend Annette Strauss was elected at-large. Jerry Rucker, the eventual winner in the other at-large post, was in a runoff. Paul Fielding had managed to get into a runoff with the incumbent Ricardo Medrano, who represented West Dallas and much of Oak Lawn. Both Ricardo and his brother Robert, who was then on the Dallas School Board, would later become my friends. In neighboring districts, Dean Vanderbilt in Lake Highlands and Far North Dallas and Craig Holcomb in East Dallas were in runoffs but would eventually win.

I made peace with the North Dallas Chamber of Commerce and served on their board of directors.

Inauguration day, shortly after the runoff elections was enjoyable. The mayor and all council members sat with their spouses on a large stage outside of City Hall. There were prayers, music, and a swearing in for the next term. I sat there, day dreaming about what would happen next and what this new phase of my life would bring.

When the ceremonies were over the Council had their first meeting and we had two items of business. The mayor was to appoint committees and committee chairs and we had to elect a mayor pro tem and a deputy mayor pro tem. The mayor pro tem chairs Council meetings when the mayor is absent and when he and the mayor are both absent the deputy mayor pro tem takes over. Both positions afforded private offices and assistants within the mayor's office.

The first order of business was these two elections. Since it involved personnel, that part was behind closed doors in executive session. Fred Blair had been the deputy so he was the logical one to move up and was unanimously elected the mayor pro tem. Jerry Rucker and my new friend Annette Strauss were both nominated for the deputy position. My vote counting before the meeting showed five votes for Jerry and five votes for Annette. I cast the deciding vote for Annette and Jerry never forgot it.

The mayor appointed committees and committee chairs. I had asked to chair the Finance Committee, but that went to Dean as it should have, him being the former budget director. I ended up chairing the Transportation Committee which was a better fit, given the traffic problems in my district and my intentions to give our drivers some relief.

Craig Holcomb, East Dallas and Dean Vanderbilt, Lake Highlands and Far North Dallas and I formed a study group people called the "Gang of Three." Over the next four years, every Wednesday that the Council met, we met for breakfast at the Farmer's Grill near City Hall to go over the agenda and share ideas.

The *Dallas Times Herald* ran a short story about the three of us and the Farmer's Grill. The cook told the reporter that he would start our orders when we walked in the door because we each ordered the same thing every time. The waitress taking our orders was only a gesture. They took our picture sitting there one morning while we were deep in discussion about something. Until the Farmer's Grill closed decades later, our picture hung in the entrance above the cash register.

The three of us became good friends and allies. We were in the middle of a divided Council and found ourselves the swing votes on just about every issue that was controversial and divisive. What did the Gang of Three accomplish during the next four years?

- We campaigned hard for the successful passage of a 1% sales tax to create Dallas Area Rapid Transit (DART) for Dallas and eventually thirteen of its suburbs.

- After enlisting the aid of the editorial boards of the two major newspapers for the area we beat back an effort by the city manager to raise tax rates, even after the tax base had grown substantially. For the two terms that I served, city tax rates were not raised.

- We helped in passing by the Council of a new planning and zoning classification system, which effectively back zoned major problem classifications.

- We engineered millions of dollars in transportation improvements, primarily for North Dallas, to be included in the 1985 city bond program and worked for its successful passage.

- We schemed with Dallas's two African-American council members to achieve the election of Richard Knight, who was eminently qualified to manage the city, as the new city manager the first African-American to hold that post.

- We negotiated several compromises of controversial zoning cases that came before the council.

- All of our districts bordered North Central Expressway. We worked with the Mayor to form a citizens group, under the leadership of Walt Humman, to negotiate a solution to North Central Expressway. Under that umbrella and with the input from a transportation engineering firm, the solution was found. Cantilever the service roads over the outside lanes where the right of way is too small to widen, Problem solved.

- I served as Chair of the Regional Transportation Council of the North Central Council of Governments, on the first Board of Trustees for what is now the Trinity Railway Express, and on a National League of Cities steering committee for Transportation and Communication.

- I spent many a day and evening in Austin lobbing the Governor, the legislature and the Texas Highway Commission on behalf of funding for transportation.

After two, two-year terms several of my friends advised me not to run again, that I had everything to lose and nothing to gain. They were right. Crude oil prices dropped substantially and then prices for commercial real estate dropped as well. Most of the major and many of the minor banks were taken down by the Feds and real estate construction came to an abrupt halt.

After my two terms, Jerry Bartos ran and won and served admirably for the next three two-year terms. I have yet to run for office again, but I did chair the Board of Trustees of Dallas Metrocare Services for six years. Dallas Metrocare provides mental health and mental retardation services to the indigent.

I told the story earlier about Tom Dunning practically laughing me out of his office when I told him I was running against Betty. Years later Tom, former City of Dallas Mayor Pro Tem Domingo Garcia and City Council member Laura Miller were in a three-way race for mayor. I supported Laura and was active on her finance committee. Laura ended up winning the race in a run-off with Tom.

Jack Worley had mentioned Mildred Cox, an engineer in the Transportation Department. Mildred became director of the Transportation Department and since I was the chair of the Council Transportation Committee, we worked closely together on both transportation and land use and she was an invaluable advisor, as was Jack, on the same two subjects.

During the *Dallas Times Herald* story about the new Council's first year the mayor's quote about our gang was to call us the Whiz Kids, which we believe he meant as a compliment.